"Dan Bolin took the ball from center, dropped back in the pocket, took a step to his left to avoid a would-be tackler, and then lofted a perfect pass to a streaking wide-receiver for the game-winning touchdown in *Avoiding the Blitz*. He's one of the best!"

—JOHN A. WEBER, staff member, Campus Crusade for Christ

"As a follower of Jesus, I need encouragement and challenge from godly friends. Dan Bolin used my own memories of and fantasies about football to accomplish both. His stories are great!"

—DR. ROBERT C. ANDRINGA, president,
Coalition for Christian Colleges and Universities

AVOIDING THE BLITZ

and Other LifeLessons from Football

Dan Bolin

NAVPRESS ◐
BRINGING TRUTH TO LIFE
NavPress Publishing Group
P.O. Box 35001, Colorado Springs, Colorado 80935

The Navigators is an international Christian organization. Our mission is to reach, disciple, and equip people to know Christ and to make Him known through successive generations. We envision multitudes of diverse people in the United States and every other nation who have a passionate love for Christ, live a lifestyle of sharing Christ's love, and multiply spiritual laborers among those without Christ.

NavPress is the publishing ministry of The Navigators. NavPress publications help believers learn biblical truth and apply what they learn to their lives and ministries. Our mission is to stimulate spiritual formation among our readers.

© 1998 by Dan Bolin
ISBN 1-57683-080-2

Cover: Wood River Media, Inc. San Rafael, CA

Unless otherwise identified, all Scripture quotations in this publication are taken from the *HOLY BIBLE: NEW INTERNATIONAL VERSION* ® (NIV®). Copyright © 1973, 1978, 1984 by International Bible Society. Used by permission of Zondervan Publishing House. All rights reserved. The other version used is the *New American Standard Bible* (NASB), © The Lockman Foundation 1960, 1962, 1963, 1968, 1971, 1972, 1973, 1975, 1977;

Printed in the United States of America

1 2 3 4 5 6 7 8 9 10 11 12 13 14 15 / 05 04 03 02 01 00 99 98

DEDICATION

This book is dedicated to the wonderful people who served God faithfully as staff members at Pine Cove Christian Conference Center while I was the Executive Director, especially:

Tim Alderson
Michael Bertino
Jim Blackwelder
John Cumming
Dan Dotson
Kevin Garrity
Tracy Jager
Christi Johnson
Kiyo "Tex" Kakuda
Kathy Lawrence
June Lininger
Peggy Marks
Robert McKenzie
Brad Mercer
Sam Moreton
Ken Sutterfield
Daniel Wallace

CONTENTS

PREFACE

I assume that most of the readers of this book will be much like me. Too many responsibilities, too full a schedule, too little time, and a nagging sense that life should be more peaceful and purposeful. Instead of writing a book addressing the problems of life at the turn of the millennium and what's wrong with our world, I decided to go with the flow. My efforts are not to change the course of society (and maybe my sights are too low), but rather to provide a small opportunity for men to engage God within their hectic schedules.

The target of this book is the guy who gets up before dawn to beat the rush-hour traffic to work and has his morning scheduled in fifteen-minute windows — then power lunch, afternoon meetings, phone calls, and reports before it's time to head out to the expressway again. He arrives home after the sun has set, just in time to kiss his kids goodnight before he falls asleep watching the ball game on TV. Not much time for himself and not much time for God.

Do you recognize yourself in a guy like that? I don't expect to change your lifestyle, but I do hope to make it easier to interject some thoughts about God into the daily routine.

The people who helped me complete this manuscript should be recognized. My daughter, Haley, is a great reader and knows good stuff from bad stuff. As a middle school student she was ready and willing to give me her best (or worst) opinion of each revision.

My wife, Cay, knows how to spell, correct grammar, and most of all, encourage. She is also much better than I am at meeting deadlines. She would wait until I was watching a great football game on TV and then ask, "How much longer until the next chapter's due?" I'd tell her, "I'm doing research."

Thanks also to Steve Webb, Sue Geiman, Gary Wilde, and the rest of the NavPress team for helping make this book a reality. I pray that by reading these pages you will enjoy the stories and gain an insight or two into the truth of God's Word. Just a brief encounter with God for thirty-one days can start the process of growing closer to Him for a lifetime.

DAN BOLIN
February, 1998

INTRODUCTION

Two things were sacred in my childhood home. One was church and the other was football. My father was a high school football coach and a deacon in the Baptist church. Life revolved around the two.

Some of my earliest and best memories are of hot chocolate on cold and rainy Friday nights. There were times of jumping on the sawdust-filled blocking dummies and riding with my dad on the seven-man sled while the players pushed it around the practice field. Searching for loose change under the grandstands with my brothers was another treat. Occasionally we'd find a dime or nickel—just enough to keep us coming back to look again on next Friday's game night.

We were also in church every Sunday morning, Sunday night, and Wednesday night. Because of Sunday night church, I never saw the Wizard of Oz in one complete sitting until video was invented. I either watched the first half and left for church about the time everybody reached the Emerald City, or we hurried home after church in time to be scared by the flying monkeys. Church was a priority in our family.

Both football and Christianity have stayed with me for life. I would say I'm a recovering footballaholic. I can still watch two or three games a weekend, but if I miss one I no longer go

11

into withdrawal symptoms. Since Tom Landry left the Cowboys, life hasn't quite been the same.

I have enjoyed football as a participant and as a spectator. Sadly, I can say the same about Christianity. My goal as a Christian is, more and more, to move out of the stands and onto the playing field. This book is about becoming a player on God's first string. It is a book about moving from spectator to player and becoming a better player through more concentration and practice.

This book is also about pep talks. Before every game I've ever been a part of, the coach gathered us together and gave us his best Knute Rockne imitation. We were ready to take on the world and do the impossible. I hope this book has some pep talk in it. But even more I hope and pray that it will be filled with stories and insights that are translated into action. Pep talks provide courage and confidence, giving us the zeal to do what we know we should do but lack the courage to accomplish. The truth of God's Word can give us the strength we need to accomplish the challenges before us.

But we need more than pep talks. We need truth. So this is more than a pep-talk book. It is about the bigger goal of knowing God and serving Him. I hope that God will use the portions of Scripture I've included to spur you on to do great things for Him. But more than that I hope you come away with a better sense of who God is and what He has done for you.

Each of the following thirty-one chapters is designed to be read and reflected on in less than ten minutes. Find time in your busy schedule to read a chapter and contemplate the message of the Scripture for your life. By learning more about God

Himself you'll be motivated to serve Him with all the gifts He has given you.

Note to the Reader:

You can use this book in a variety of ways. You might choose to read a chapter a day for a month. Great! But don't limit yourself to that kind of a rigorous reading plan if your schedule would tend to make it a chore. In that case, try these options:

Read a chapter a week for thirty-one weeks, perhaps on a Saturday night before Sunday worship;
Read chapters with a group of friends and discuss your reactions and insights together—whenever you can meet;
Read before you go to a football game, during half time on TV, or whenever you *think* about football;
Or . . . just read when the Spirit moves you.

Reading this book ought to be like taking a breath of fresh air whenever you need it. So no matter how you plan your devotional times, let them become quality visits with the Lord. Pray, and meditate upon His word. That way, you'll be a first-string player on God's winning team.

ONE

Avoiding the Blitz

Someone has said that the second most important player on a football team, right behind the starting quarterback, is the backup quarterback. He never knows when he'll be called upon to step into the game and lead the team. Therefore, he must be prepared, physically and mentally, to insure the team's best possible performance should the starter leave the game.

He must also fully understand the defenses that will be thrown at him, particularly the various blitzing techniques that could drill him into the ground on key pass plays. In fact, when it comes to the passing game, victory can hinge on avoiding the blitz.

Pay Attention!

For one experienced backup quarterback, a game at mid-season was like all the others. The starting quarterback was healthy and the chances of the backup playing were slim to none. This backup had entered games before and he knew he could step up to the challenge if called upon. So during the preceding week of practice his mind drifted to other interests. He paid little attention to the films and didn't open his playbook. He suited up for the game expecting another day of wearing the headset and carrying a clipboard.

He was wrong. An injury to the starter thrust him into the action with no warning. It was a disaster from the start. The defensive schemes and blitzing attacks had been explained in practice but he had not paid attention and was totally unprepared to perform his job and lead the team. After the game he admitted his lack of preparation and was cut the next morning.

This young man lost his significant salary as well as the respect of his teammates and fans. He hadn't been ready at the moment of need. His playing time was unexpected for sure, but his job was to be ready without warning and he paid dearly for his failure.

Be Ready!

There are at least three ways Christians are expected to be constantly prepared while avoiding the daily blitzes of life. First, we are to be ready to share our faith with others. 1 Peter 3:15b says,

Always be prepared to give an answer to everyone who asks you to give the reason for the hope that you have. But do this with gentleness and respect.

Opportunities to share the gospel may appear at any moment—in a chance meeting with a stranger, when a neighbor suddenly wants to talk about eternal matters, or during a conversation with a coworker experiencing grief. We must be ready to respond without warning.

Second, we need to be ready to preach God's Word. In 2 Timothy 4:2 we read,

Preach the Word; be prepared in season and out of season; correct, rebuke and encourage—with great patience and careful instruction.

Paul was instructing Timothy, his young pastoral intern. We may not be preachers but each of us should become familiar with God's Word so that we can share a verse of encouragement with someone who is hurting, a word of warning with those who are straying, or a piece of wisdom with one who has doubts and questions. We must be ready in season—during times when we might *expect* to share, and out of season—those times when the unexpected becomes reality and we're thrust into the role of first-team quarterback.

Third, we must be ready for Christ's return. Matthew warns us,

Therefore keep watch, because you do not know on what day your Lord will come. . . . So you also must be ready, because the Son of Man will come at an hour when you do not expect him. (24:42,44)

Some day Jesus will come to the earth a second time. The first time He came as a baby; next time He'll come in all His power and glory. Perhaps we assume that because He didn't come yesterday He won't come today. That assumption has worked well for 2,000 years, but one of these days . . . .

We know that God is long-suffering and He goes well beyond our endurance point when it comes to patience. But we mistake His long-suffering for an "I don't care" attitude. Because He generally doesn't judge our sin immediately, we may begin to think that He never will. In fact, He is patiently withholding judgment, waiting for more people to turn to Him.

It's worth saying again: *Be prepared.* We must expect the unexpected—the blitzes of life—and be ready to explain the hope that is in us, share the Word, and live our lives to please Him when He arrives unexpectedly. In all these ways we can avoid the blitz and get on with our push toward the heavenly goal.

EXTRA POINTS
READ EPHESIANS 5:15-20

- What kinds of blitzes will you need to avoid in the coming weeks? What can you do now to prepare for upcoming opportunities?
- What things about your life would you want to change if you knew Christ would return today?

TWO

ESSENTIAL EQUIPMENT

HAVE YOU BEEN IN THE STANDS WHEN THERE IS A SUDDEN HUSH OF the crowd? The ominous silence descends occasionally when a helmet flies off in the middle of a play. A gasp rises from the stands and the action on the field becomes instantly less critical than the question, "Will the guy live through this play?"

Without the necessary equipment the game becomes dangerous. The better the protection, though, the more likely the players will throw their bodies into the contest with reckless abandon. Yet, with all of their equipment in place, football players look like monsters. Adding helmets, shoulder pads, and hip pads to their already oversized frames—and then finishing the outfit with knee pads, elbow pads, and in some cases flack jackets—makes even ordinary players appear superhuman.

And why not? We fans expect them to perform superhuman feats. Our team's players ought to run faster, tackle harder, block better, and kick farther than any opponent.

Equipped for the Fight?
We Christians are expected to do superhuman tasks as well. To protect us from the crashing blows that this world can deliver and to help us withstand the dangers of living in our threatening culture, God has provided essential protective

19

equipment. Ephesians 6:10-11 states,

> *Finally, be strong in the Lord and in his mighty power. Put on the full armor of God so that you can take your stand against the devil's schemes.*

The passage goes on to describe six pieces of equipment that all members of God's team should wear for their protection and the freedom to enter the game with enthusiasm.

First, we buckle the *belt of truth* around our waists. We tend to believe half truths about ourselves and about our world: we're either too bad or too good; the world's out of control or totally programmed; God directs every decision or He's completely absent. In reality, our security resides in God's truth as it binds together every aspect of our lives in wisdom and balance. Without that solid undergirding, we trade the clarity of God's truth for the distortion of our own perspectives.

Next is the *breastplate of righteousness.* Our protection is tied directly to our exercise of character. When we behave without a commitment to righteousness we open ourselves to the dangers of this world.

It's better to charge forward in the shoes of *the readiness that comes from the gospel of peace.* A sprained ankle, broken toe, or bruised sole can sideline any player. Worry, guilt, shame, and fear destroy our personal peace while conflict, envy, anger, and gossip attack the harmony among team members. When we are at peace with ourselves and with others, however, we can serve the Prince of Peace effectively.

Then the *shield of faith* will ward off the doubts, distractions, and temptations that come winging toward us at the worst possible moments. Simple trust is a powerful source of strength.

Finally, *the helmet of salvation* protects the nerve center of our lives. Our thought processes and our sensory perceptions are protected by our helmet. We need that head gear, because when we come to the end of our rope we tend to make irrational and silly decisions. In 1 Peter 4:7, the apostle says, "The end of all things is near. Therefore be clear minded and self-controlled so that you can pray." When we feel as though the world is crashing down around us, it's great to know that our helmet of salvation protects us so we can think clearly, remain self-controlled, and turn to God with our whole being.

Put It On!

Knowing that our salvation is secure gives us freedom to face the dangers of this life with confidence. No blow of the enemy is stronger than the love of Christ, the One who fits us with salvation's eternal protection.

God has provided us with great equipment but we need to put it on. We may think we can enter the game without God's provision or that we will be encumbered by it. Nothing could be further from the truth. Put it on. Be protected by it and use its power to make a difference in the lives of those around you.

EXTRA POINTS
READ COLOSSIANS 3:5-10

- Are there times when you lack confidence as a Christian?
- Which piece of equipment do you need the most at those times? How would you actually "use" it in daily life?

THREE

BEWARE THOSE PERSONAL FOULS

THE REFEREES MAY HAVE THE TOUGHEST JOB ON THE FIELD. THEY deal with hulking bodies crashing into each other at top speed, huge piles of angry players scrambling and pushing for extra yardage, and all the deceptive tactics built into the fabric of the game. The stands overflow with screaming fans who think they know all the rules and they expect each technical, procedural, and behavioral regulation to be applied to their team's advantage.

Naturally, the technical and procedural rules are the least controversial. Either too many men stand on the field or not; a player lines up offsides or behind the line; a formation is either legal or illegal. The difficult decisions revolve around the more subjective personal fouls. Holding, pass interference, unsportsmanlike conduct — those are the calls requiring great eyesight and quick judgment.

Playing a whole game without a penalty is a rare feat, but the team suffering the least penalty yards has a great advantage. A long run called back because of holding quickly deflates the whole team. But picking up a first down on pass interference adds fuel to any scoring drive.

Moving Forward?

Avoiding the setback of penalties is critical to moving forward in any life endeavor. Even in ancient times the principle held true. Deuteronomy 17:16-19, for example, provides directives for the Israelite kings regarding certain "infractions" to avoid. The directives are simple and to the point. For example:

The king, moreover, must not acquire great numbers of horses for himself . . . He must not take many wives, or his heart will be led astray. He must not accumulate large amounts of silver and gold.

These commands were directed toward folks who lived long ago, but they speak to all of us today, especially those in leadership. If we're called for a penalty in one of these areas it could devastate our lives.

The first command has to do with power. During biblical times the horse, as a weapon, provided a significant technical advantage in warfare. The horsemen or charioteers were far superior to the foot soldiers. Horses were faster, more maneuverable, carried more weapons, and struck terror into the enemy. A king who amassed a huge stable of horses might soon lose his sense of dependence on the Lord for protection and power. The more "horse power," the less relevant God's power.

The power we acquire can undermine our own dependence upon God. Our title at work, our position in the church, our level of education, and access to information—all are sources of personal power. As God provides opportunities for leadership we must constantly ask ourselves, "Am I trusting God or am I trusting the things He has entrusted to me?"

The second personal foul that can send our lives backwards is immorality. Ancient kings usually had the money and power to take many wives and concubines. Some of the wives merely ratified political or economic alliances, but mostly the women of the harem were there to satisfy every sexual impulse. Pleasure and reputation were at the heart of the king's self-centered sexual indulgence.

Sexual sins can destroy our family, our reputation, and even our health. The warning to the king is a warning to each of us. Stray in this area and be prepared to pay a heavy price. When life gets tough and tension fills our days, we look for something—anything—to make the pain go away and divert our minds from the problems before us. The king certainly had his share of headaches, but his soul was to find contentment in his eternal relationship with the Lord. That solution would be so much better than settling for the temporary thrill of the next beautiful harem acquisition.

When do you experience the most gut-wrenching pressures? How do you handle the inevitable pull to escapist comforts? The challenges and responsibilities of life can twist us into knots, but we must guard ourselves from sensual stimulation that fans the flame of elicit sexual impulses. The joy and satisfaction of a marriage relationship must not be cheapened, weakened, or obliterated by immorality.

The third personal foul that can push us back is greed. The Israelite kings were to avoid amassing great amounts of silver and gold. They were responsible for the economic well-being of the nation and were to be just and fair in their personal financial dealings. In other words, why accumulate vast amounts of treasure just to have a stockpile rising higher than a neighbor's? Taxation that merely filled the storehouses created civil dissatisfaction. The people would grow unhappy, ripe for insurrection. Therefore, as the treasury grew, so grew the possibility of a foreign power attempting a conquest. The more gold and silver, the greater the threat to the nation, internally and externally. If our self-worth moves up and down with the stock market, we have placed our security in silver and gold. Greed has replaced godliness as a basis for our strength.

Avoid the Penalties

Weapons, women, and wealth have their place. The king wasn't told to disband his army, divorce the queen, or give away all his money. But all posed a threat if not treated with care and kept in proper balance.

We too must approach these areas of life with wisdom and caution. Let us avoid every potential penalty—especially the devastating personal fouls that come with misusing our power, our sexuality, and our money.

EXTRA POINTS
READ PHILIPPIANS 4:8

- What is the difference between proper and improper desires for power, sex, and money in our lives today?
- What signals in your life indicate that you might be getting out of balance in any of these areas?

FOUR

EXTRA POINTS

WE WERE AHEAD, BUT ONLY BY ONE POINT, AS WE LINED UP FOR OUR opponent's extra point attempt. The game was as good as tied, but if there is a level of play where extra points aren't automatic, it's junior-varsity football.

Hope was still alive.

The football sat in front of the uprights as I positioned myself in the gap directly between the offensive center and the left guard. Then, as the ball spiraled back, I lunged forward. The center blocked right and the guard blocked left, turning me sideways, twisting me awkwardly.

But my head ended up in just the right place at just the right time.

Yes, the ball slammed off the side of my helmet. I would like to say that this skillful little maneuver saved our victory. In reality, the kick was so low it had no hope of getting over the crossbar anyway.

And perhaps skill was less a part of the equation than my memories keep trying to make it.

The Reward: More Opportunities

Usually, extra points are rather routine events. The crowd is still buzzing with the excitement of the touchdown while the

26

special team members run onto the field to go through the motions of the extra-point conversion. Kickers so rarely miss that we think of touchdowns as seven points.

As routine as they are, though, extra points do represent a great principle of life: The reward for success is the opportunity for more success. Teams that never score touchdowns never have the chance to attempt extra points, while those frequently in the end zone give their kicker lots of chances to add to the score.

Jesus told a parable in Matthew 25 that illustrates this principle. It has to do with three servants whose master entrusted them with talents—amounts of money—while he was away on a trip. The three were to use their different amounts effectively in the master's absence and report their earnings when he returned.

When the master returned for his audit of the funds, the first servant had doubled his five talents and now had ten. The second had also been successful, doubling his initial two talents to report a total of four. The final servant, who had originally received only one talent, was next in line—with his palms becoming very sweaty. He had done nothing with his money and now the day of reckoning had arrived.

In verse 25 he says, *"So I was afraid and went out and hid your talent in the ground. See, here is what belongs to you."*

The master replies in verses 27-28, *"Well then, you should have put my money on deposit with the bankers, so that when I returned I would have received it back with*

*interest. Take the talent from him and give it to the one
who has the ten talents."*

This parable deals with the nation of Israel and its religious
leaders, those who had been entrusted with a unique understanding of God. God had chosen Israel as a special people to
be a light to the rest of the world. But instead of being a passionate missionary nation spreading the message of God's love
to the world, the Israelites kept this treasure all to themselves.
While hoarding God's bounty, they lost it.

The principle holds true throughout life. The reward for
faithful service is more opportunity for service. If you perform
well, you will be given the chance to apply your gifts time and
time again.

The fearful and lazy servant lost his talent and the servant
who started with five ended with eleven. But I wonder about
the middle servant who began with two and doubled his allotment just as the first servant did. Yet he didn't share in the
bonus talent. Why didn't he, too, get a portion of the lazy servant's blunder? Why did it all go to the first servant?

The Challenge: Keep Growing

Perhaps the answer comes in verse 15, where it says that the talents were distributed to the men, "each according to his ability."
The two talents given to the middle servant were only slightly
more than the amount entrusted to the fearful servant. This
second servant had shown some ability but was not an experienced veteran. The five-talent servant was a sure bet, and the
master knew that the bulk of his treasure would be in good
hands.

I think most of us are two-talent servants. We don't possess the greatest gifts and abilities and we haven't always performed to the level that we know we should. But we can keep growing and improving. We can keep seeking opportunities to serve God and to please Him.

And God wants us to keep working hard. Maybe next time He'll grant us three or four talents and check on how we handle that responsibility. When we execute well and put six points on the board, the opportunities for extra points are sure to follow.

EXTRA POINTS
READ 1 CORINTHIANS 12:4-12

- In what ways are you serving God with your gifts and abilities these days?
- What indications do you have that some talents might be staying hidden? What things could you do to "dig them up" again?

FIVE

HOW'S THE WEATHER?

GROWING UP IN OREGON, I HAVE ALWAYS ROOTED FOR THE DUCKS of the University of Oregon and the Oregon State Beavers. Imagine that, Ducks and Beavers. One state gifted with two great mascots.

In 1996 the Ducks earned a trip to Dallas' Cotton Bowl on New Year's Day. The Cotton Bowl is less than two hours from my home in Tyler, and my friends Doug and Bonnie Thompson gave me four great tickets.

One ticket was for me, one for my wife, Cay. My daughter, Haley, got ticket number three while my friend Roger Rodgers from Houston was on board to use the fourth ticket. We had great expectations for the Quack Attack. Even though Colorado was a big favorite, I kept my hopes alive for an upset victory.

As game day approached we began to watch the extended weather forecasts. The closer we got to the game, the worse the outlook. And for once the weatherman was right: cold, rain, wind . . . a perfect day for ducks.

It turned out to be a perfect day for Buffaloes. Colorado trounced Oregon.

The real story wasn't the game; it was the attendance. The weather kept some people home—the ones with good sense—because the Cotton Bowl, without a Texas team hosting it, just wasn't as appealing as staying inside and watching several great games on TV. Feasting with friends in a warm house while channel-surfing several games is tough to beat.

So there were lots of empty seats when the game began and by half time the stadium was nearly empty. Cay and Haley went to the car, along with the vast majority of those who had shown up for the opening kickoff. By the end of the game the stadium was empty.

Except for Roger, me, the wind, the rain, and the bitter cold.

We expected it to be bad, but not this bad. The Ducks were beaten badly, the weather was beyond miserable, and a nagging question kept rolling around in the back of my head: *Should I be learning something from all these empty seats?*

In Stormy Weather . . .

We expect life to be tough but not *this* tough. We suffer terrible defeats, the climate of our lives can turn truly miserable, and we look around wondering, "Does everyone else know something I don't?"

During Jesus' last night with His disciples, He encouraged them by sharing some key words of wisdom:

> *"I have told you these things, so that in me you may have peace. In this world you will have trouble. But take heart! I have overcome the world."* (John 16:33)

This verse is filled with ointment to soothe our wounds in this world. There are three parts to the healing cream.

First, the words *in me you may have peace* tell of the only reliable source of peace available. Jesus was intentional about

His time with the disciples. Facing the difficult hours and days ahead, they would require resources beyond their human capacities. Peace wouldn't reside in the circumstances of life but in the relationship with their Lord.

The world is a tough place. *You will have trouble here* throughout your days. Tension invades the key relationships of our lives, and work often drains our creativity, leaving us frustrated and exhausted. There is no escape. Rich and poor, young and old find trouble constantly knocking at the door. Yes, we want to live in a trouble-free world; instead, the challenge is to live with God's peace in a trouble-filled world.

Christ knew the destructive power of incessant problems grinding against the peace of His presence. He thus reminds the disciples, *Take heart! I have overcome the world.* In this promise we can stay positive and keep focused on the ultimate victory that will eventually set all things right.

The score may indeed go against us, the weather will often be stormy, and those around us may know things we don't. But victory comes through peace with Jesus. Get to know Him. And enjoy the calm of living with this confidence.

EXTRA POINTS
READ JOHN 14:27

- What things tend to keep you awake at night?
- Would you rather have a hassle-free life, or problems that develop godly character? Why?

STAYING BETWEEN THE LINES

My FATHER, THE HIGH SCHOOL FOOTBALL COACH, INCLUDED HIS young sons in his work. It was wonderful! In some of my earliest memories I'm shagging footballs, attacking blocking dummies, and holding clipboards on the sidelines. During the last days of summer, two-a-day practices consumed our family's time and attention. My brothers and I got up early, Mom packed a lunch, and we always came home late for dinner. Most of the time we boys were just underfoot, but occasionally we were given chores to earn our keep.

Drill after drill could teach the new team only so much, so during the second week of practice a full scrimmage was planned. The squad broke into two teams and a makeshift playing area was laid out on the practice field. There were no sidelines, no end zones, no yard markers, and the coaches acted as the officials. To give the game a sense of reality, the first-down markers were used along the edge of the field. Two of the injured players held the ends of the chains and I was given the down marker that indicated how far the ball had moved on each play.

With no lines on the field, forward progress was an estimate at best. No matter where I placed the down marker, the players on offense said I was too stingy, and the defenders figured I was favoring the ball carrier. I couldn't seem to satisfy anyone.

What Are the Rules Around Here?

Without lines on a football field there can be no objective standard by which to play the game. And without objective standards to give our lives guidance and structure we will rationalize our actions to condone purely self-centered impulses.

One of the lowest points in the life of ancient Israel came at the end of the period of the judges. The nation had produced cycles of rebellion, punishment, and repentance for hundreds of years, but now the rebellion had resulted in civil war among the tribes. The final statement of the book of Judges describes this dark period of Israel's history:

Everyone did as he saw fit. (21:25)

Isn't it the same in our society today? Without clear moral standards, people make up the rules as they go along. If it feels good, do it. Take the course of least resistance. In this environment, truth becomes whatever we want it to be.

Yet, the boundaries of this life flow from the Scriptures. In Psalm 19:7-10 David tells us how God's Word can keep us in bounds. At the conclusion of this section he writes,

By them is your servant warned; in keeping them there is great reward. (Verse 11)

There are two benefits to having lines on the field of life: the warnings and the rewards. The warnings have to do with boundaries and structure. The sidelines tell the players, "This far and no farther." There is plenty of room to play on the field, but if they go out of bounds the play stops and they have to start over. The same is true in our daily lives. We have a great deal of freedom within the confines that God has laid out for us.

The simplest summary of the boundary lines comes through in Matthew 22:37-39. Jesus is replying to a question as to what is the greatest commandment. He says,

> *"'Love the Lord your God with all your heart and with all your soul and with all your mind.' This is the first and greatest commandment. And the second is like it: 'Love your neighbor as yourself.'"*

If we live within these two boundaries—loving God and loving people—we will experience success and satisfaction. Outside of these lines is danger and the play gets stopped.

Rewards flow from staying inside the lines. Without yard lines and goal lines, we would have no way of judging our progress. But as we evaluate our lives in light of God's Word we can see areas of improvement as well as issues of concern. We can fix our eyes on the goal and move toward it with assurance that we are heading in the right direction. Such confidence is a wonderful reward in itself. Do you have it?

EXTRA POINTS
READ MATTHEW 5:18-19

- In what areas of your life are you seeing spiritual progress?
- What actions or attributes in your life are coming close to being "out of bounds"?

SEVEN

FOOTBALL ... OR SWITZERLAND?

IN THE 1960S, PROFESSIONAL FOOTBALL WAS STILL LOOKING FOR respect. It was growing in popularity but hadn't risen to the prominent place in American culture that it enjoys today. But on November 17, 1968, the New York Jets and Oakland Raiders played a rather memorable game. With one minute and three seconds remaining, it was 32 to 29 in favor of the Jets.

Then came the fateful decision.

The TV execs felt ratings would best be served by cutting away from an almost-concluded football game and allowing viewers to see the entire feature film "Heidi." Naturally, diehard fans lit up the station's phone lines with their fuming, pouting, and complaining. They wanted to see the game through to the very last second. But after all, it was almost over, and the broadcasters remained firm.

What those fans missed was one of the greatest come-from-behind victories in NFL history. The Raiders scored two touchdowns in the last 42 seconds and surged ahead to win, 43 to 32.

All this while the nation's football fanatics "enjoyed" the story of a cute little girl in frilly dresses flitting through the glorious scenery of Switzerland's high country. . . .

Another Missed Comeback

This wasn't the first time a great victory went unseen. It happened in the Old Testament book of Jonah. Most of us know the story of Jonah and the whale, but we may not be as familiar with what happened after Jonah and the huge fish parted company.

After cleaning himself up, Jonah traveled to the city of Nineveh, the capital of Israel's archenemies, the Assyrians. God told the reluctant prophet to preach to the city and to tell the people they'd be destroyed in forty days. So that's what he did.

Jonah must have been a pretty good preacher because his messages sparked a revival that spread throughout the city. The people even declared a fast to focus on the spiritual issues in their lives. They put on sackcloth to show the depth of their sorrow and the king himself joined in, sitting in the dust to show his humility before Jonah's God. Ordering even the animals to join the fast, the king urged a renunciation of all evil and violence.

And God accepted the people's response. After all, the reason He'd sent Jonah in the first place was to generate this repentant spirit in the Ninevites. Jonah 3:10 says,

When God saw what they did and how they turned from their evil ways, he had compassion and did not bring upon them the destruction he had threatened.

God had accomplished His plan except for one small detail—transforming Jonah's heart. The next verse is Jonah's response to God's mercy and grace:

But Jonah was greatly displeased and became angry. (4:1)

I'm not sure why Jonah responded the way he did. It's true that the Ninevites had been bitter enemies of Israel, and no doubt Jonah hoped they would be destroyed, making him the hero of his homeland. And certainly his reputation as a prophet was on the line. If the calamity he predicted didn't occur, his peers could discredit him. Whatever the reason, Jonah was not happy.

The story goes on to say that Jonah was so upset that he wanted to die. He took up watch on the city, hoping that God would destroy his enemies and make him look good to his friends. In his anger Jonah says,

I knew that you are a gracious and compassionate God, slow to anger and abounding in love, a God who relents from sending calamity. (4:2)

When revival broke out, God was eager to show His love to the Ninevites. Jonah wasn't so eager.

And that's ironic, because in his experience with the fish, Jonah knew the grace and compassion of the Lord firsthand. He'd been as good as dead. But now he was upset by a merciful God who was willing to root for another underdog.

Stay Tuned In

So Jonah missed enjoying one of the greatest comeback victories of all time. His selfish, hardened heart sharply contrasted with God's tender concern. The prophet should have been tearing down the goal post, delighting in a victory celebration with people whose chances had suddenly been restored. Instead he pouted and complained, wishing for God's judgment to fall on anyone but himself.

It's easy to miss what God is doing in our lives and in the lives of others. We must stayed tuned to Him to see and appreciate the victories He's creating all around us.

I like to think that Jonah had a change of heart later in life. Although Scripture doesn't tell us he reformed, my guess is that he wrote the small book that bears his name in order to warn others of the dangers of running from God and of the silliness of missing some pretty fantastic reversals.

EXTRA POINTS
READ 1 JOHN 1:8-10

- What exciting turnaround has God done in your heart?
- Why are we eager to accept God's grace toward ourselves but often hesitant to extend the same graciousness to those around us?

EIGHT

THE MAN HIMSELF

I WAS TRYING TO PUT AS MUCH ON MY PLATE AS POSSIBLE WITHOUT looking too hoggish in front of the rest of the family. It was Mother's Day, 1982, and as I picked through the shrimp at a huge buffet table (searching for the largest ones), I glanced across the table at another man with salad tongs in his hands.

Actually, it was *the* man himself: Tom Landry.

Please understand. I grew up as a wild-eyed Dallas fan. I can't say the Cowboys deserved the title "America's Team," but they certainly were "My Team." I covered my bedroom walls with team posters and slept on a Dallas Cowboy pillowcase every night. Sunday afternoons were committed to supporting my heroes with total focus and undying devotion.

The man across the shrimp looked just like the television version of Coach Landry, but he was much bigger than I had expected. I'm 6 foot 4 and he looked me straight in the eye.

Distorted Perspective?

When I'd watched him on the sidelines standing next to Harvey Martin and Too Tall Jones, the coach looked 5' 10" at best. The optical illusion resulted from the size of those standing around him, huge players who significantly distorted my perspective.

Landry was as tall as ever, but my perception was way off base.

The Bible speaks of three dangerous illusions that distort our perspectives in life. The first is the illusion of our own importance. We tend to think the universe ought to revolve around us while family and friends bend their schedules, priorities, expectations, and resources to meet our needs. We call it being assertive, but perceptive observers may recognize our deep need for control, possibly born of feelings of inadequacy and insecurity. Matthew 23:11-12 states,

> *"The greatest among you will be your servant. For whoever exalts himself will be humbled, and whoever humbles himself will be exalted."*

We can be pretty tactless in avoiding this call to humility. We keep trying to promote ourselves by denying our weaknesses or overcompensating for them. We present an image much like the Wizard of Oz—all pomp and bluster—but the man "behind the curtain" is rather weak and helpless. Nevertheless, we work harder and harder to present an image we think will make us popular, powerful, and successful.

The second illusion that warps our view of the world has to do with our problems. When we're in the midst of a trying time, it's easy to be overwhelmed with the magnitude of the problem. Our emotions can become so sensitive that we magnify normal concerns into enormous crises. Have you noticed how that can happen, especially at night? I am a worrier. If I have an average-sized worry when I go to bed, it can spawn a howling monster by two in the morning. I think of biblical

David as a warrior rather than a worrier, but in Psalm 30:5 he seems to describe the situation I've faced too many times:

Weeping may remain for a night,
but rejoicing comes in the morning.

The distortion of my problems ties me up in knots during the darkness of the night. But when morning comes it brings with it a more accurate perspective and more realistic hope for resolution.

A distorted view of ourselves and a distorted understanding of our problems stem from the third and most destructive illusion we face: an inaccurate view of God Himself. We may think that God is playing a cosmic game of hide-and-seek, keeping His identity and attributes hidden from us. But nothing could be further from the truth.

Get a Clearer View

Over the centuries God has revealed Himself to human beings through dreams, angels, prophets, and even a donkey. On the first Palm Sunday, even the rocks would have delivered God's message if the people hadn't sung Hosanna. But three readily available sources of divine revelation allow us to gain a clear view of God's character and love for us. First, He uses nature to tell us things about Himself. Psalm 19:1 says, "The heavens declare the glory of God."

The whole of creation reveals the Creator. By examining God's creation we can know something of His majesty, power, eternality, wisdom, and glory. Any willing observer can "look through" the mountains, stars, rivers, and flowers to see the God who made them all.

However, what we know of God indirectly through His creation must be combined with the direct revelation of God's Word. He actually wrote us a letter to tell us all about Himself. We can read it and study it to know Him better and better.

The final and greatest means of revelation is found in God's Son. Hebrews 1:2-3 states,

In these last days he has spoken to us by his Son, whom he appointed heir of all things, and through whom he made the universe. The Son is the radiance of God's glory and the exact representation of his being . . .

To see God without distortion we must look at His Son. We can know His glory through creation; we can know how to please Him through studying His written Word. But we know Him personally through Jesus.

And remember—the Man Himself is much bigger than you might expect. The more your perspective changes and you realize how "big" He really is, the closer you get to Him.

EXTRA POINTS
READ JOB 36:22-33

- In what areas of your life do you sometimes experience a distorted perspective?
- What tends to limit your view of the greatness of God? What things help you overcome this problem?

NINE

LEARN THAT PLAYBOOK

FRESHMAN FOOTBALL BEGAN AFTER A TOUGH DAY NEGOTIATING MY way through brand-new hallways and facing a mountain of challenging assignments. The first event was a meeting in the locker room with guys who all looked as though they'd been shaving for years. We made small talk and tough talk until a coach arrived and a hush settled on this expectant group of would-be Heisman Trophy winners. Rules were laid down in no uncertain terms. The use and misuse of equipment was explained, physical examinations were detailed, forms were signed. And then we each received a little blue binder with a number in the top right-hand corner.

It was a rather crude document by today's standards. It had dark-blue mimeograph ink, crooked letters, and jagged streaks where the master had creased during printing. But to us ninth-grade football players, this hallowed volume was absolutely sacrosanct.

It was THE PLAYBOOK.

It safeguarded twelve pages of grid-iron treasure: top-secret plays, ingenious strategies, and all our special rules. We were responsible for learning everything in it before the next day, keeping it with us always, referring to it daily throughout the season. And we knew that something quite terrible would happen to the first poor soul who dared lose this precious tome.

Knowing What's Expected

The playbook explained what the coach expected of us and how to best fulfill his assignments. The more we read and studied, the more we understood what he wanted from his players. We gained insights into what he valued and expected, because the more we studied the book, the better we knew him.

The playbook for the Christian is the Word of God. Paul reminds us that,

> *All Scripture is God-breathed and is useful for teaching, rebuking, correcting and training in righteousness, so that the man of God may be thoroughly equipped for every good work.* (2 Timothy 3:16-17)

The source, the uses, and the result of the Christian's playbook are captured in these verses. As for the source, we know that the Bible is God-breathed. Books have been written about what those words actually mean, but for most of us it's simply enough to recognize that God initiated the communication. He had something to say to us about who He is and what He expects from our lives. He isn't playing a cosmic game of hide-and-seek but has provided all the information we need to live lives that please Him.

Four functional uses of Scripture come through here: teaching, rebuking, correcting, and instructing in righteousness. *Teaching* from God's Word is fundamental for Christian growth and maturity. A new Christian, excited about serving God, needs the truth of God's Word to channel energy and activity into productive areas of service. Without sound teaching from the Word, error can creep into the life of any believer. A good church, Christian radio, Christian books, and small groups are all important as long as they are providing solid teaching from the Word of God.

When believers ignore teaching from God's Word, they may need *rebuking*. Most of us would rather mind our own business and avoid the conflict that might accompany rebuke. Fortunately, the task of rebuking is the job of the Word of God. Our job is to apply the proper biblical principles—in a spirit of love, humility, and good will—to the circumstances facing an erring believer. Using the Word of God to confront a sinful situation is the most healthy method of resolving a difficult problem in the body of Christ.

After rebuking a fellow believer, *correcting* him or her is the next step. We certainly aren't going to blast away with both barrels, demolishing the sinful person. For we ourselves are sinners, too. Therefore we confront the situation in a way that leads to repentance and renewal before God—for all involved. The goal is to restore the needy one to a life of godliness.

This process culminates in *training in righteousness*. We are to be trained to live righteous lives that honor and serve God. We receive our training as we learn and apply biblical truths. The process begins and ends, then, in God's Word, for that is where we discover His plan for us to please Him throughout our lives.

For the Right Result

The two words "so that" are critical to understanding these short verses. God provides instruction for living our lives with a purpose bigger than pure self-interest and more important than mere intellectual stimulation. The result of our time in God's Word is to equip us to serve our Master effectively. We must put into practice the things we learn in order to influence our world for Him. We are to use the truth of God's Word to reach out to neighbors and to strengthen our fellow believers. The areas of service will be unique to each Christian, but the result of our Bible study must always be good works.

When we young football players received our playbook, we weren't evaluated on how well we remembered each offensive formation and every defensive set. We were judged by how many games we won or lost. This wasn't fantasy football for sideline commentators. *We learned the playbook in order to play the game.* In the same way, we're called to learn the Word of God in order to enter the game and make a difference for the cause of Christ.

EXTRA POINTS
READ HEBREWS 4:12

- How could you restructure your days or weeks in order to receive more input from God's Word?
- What is the biggest "so that" in your life? Where is the Word of God making the most impact on how you live?

TEN

BIGGER THAN LIFE?

THE DAY BEFORE FOOTBALL PRACTICE BEGAN, WE MET TO RECEIVE our equipment and to be weighed and measured. I tipped the scales at 180 pounds that summer before my senior year in high school and I stood 5 feet 10 inches tall. I had just turned seventeen, but it would be two years before I'd reach 6'4".

A few days before our season opener we got a preview of the program to be sold at the games that season. My teammates and I were amazed as we scanned the listed sizes of our players. My high school coach believed in psychological warfare. The more over-six-foot, over-200-pound players in the program, the greater the intimidation factor. We wanted to appear as big as possible, so the size numbers were inflated. I was listed as six feet tall and 200 pounds. A lot of us had seemingly put on weight for the program.

Fabricating Protection

The difference between our real sizes and our supposedly scarier proportions wasn't so great. But the fact that our dimensions were "fudged" at all was significant in our minds—especially since high school football was supposed to have something to do with "character building."

In our own daily lives we often want to appear bigger than we really are. But each time we "bear false witness" we betray hunger for protection, possessions, or inordinate popularity.

First consider the protection aspect. The biblical Abraham was a powerful Bedouin shepherd, but he was no match for an established king, especially on the king's home turf. Twice Abraham encountered situations in which he feared for his life and was willing to compromise the truth for the sake of his personal safety. Sarah, his wife, was very beautiful and would have made a wonderful addition to a sultan's harem. When Abraham arrived in the town of Gerar, he told people that Sarah was his sister. This was a half truth because Sarah was his half-sister. A king might kill a husband to gain a widow for his harem but a brother was safe. In Genesis 20:2-3 we read:

> *Abraham said of his wife Sarah, "She is my sister." Then Abimelech king of Gerar sent for Sarah and took her. But God came to Abimelech in a dream one night and said to him, "You are as good as dead because of the woman you have taken; she is a married woman."*

Abraham was willing to compromise the truth to gain protection, but in so doing he compromised his own character and put Sarah in a horrible predicament. Any of us might seek protection from consequences by telling only our side of the story, by shading the account to make us look good and cast others in a negative light. Yet each time we do this we wither just a little more inside.

Craving Possessions

Gehazi was the servant of the great prophet Elisha. He had seen God accomplish amazing feats through Elisha and was no stranger to the miracles surrounding Elisha's life. One situation was particularly tempting for Gehazi. Naaman, the general of the army of Aram, had contracted leprosy and had no hope of recovery. Following a long-shot lead, he came to Elisha seeking a cure, and the prophet commanded him to bathe in the Jordan River seven times. He did so and was healed.

As you can imagine, the general was overjoyed. He offered Elisha the moon — gold, silver, fine clothes, food, and anything else Elisha might have asked for. However, Elisha refused any compensation and sent Naaman back to Aram.

This frustrated and upset Gehazi. All that wealth and none of it for him! Once the general's caravan was out of Elisha's sight, Gehazi ran after it and told Naaman that visitors had just arrived and that Elisha had reconsidered. The prophet now needed silver and two sets of clothes to properly greet and entertain his guests. Naaman eagerly obliged and Gehazi took the gifts and hid them for himself.

But the greedy servant didn't get away with his plan. God revealed the situation to Elisha and he confronted Gehazi upon his return. His punishment was to acquire his own case of leprosy. In other words, Gehazi traded his integrity for possessions and got much more in the deal than he had bargained for.

Buying Popularity

Ananias and Sapphira were members of the early church who had witnessed the praise and honor that Barnabas had received when he sold a piece of real estate and gave the proceeds to the church. They too had a piece of property and decided to contribute the sale price to the church.

But they didn't want to give it all. They wanted to be well thought of and also receive the same honor that Barnabas had received; they just didn't want to give up all the money. And that was fine; they had the right to do whatever they wanted with the proceeds of the sale.

Yet they tried to have their cake and eat it too. After selling the land, they set aside a portion of the proceeds for themselves and brought the remainder to the church, presenting it to the elders as though the gift were the full price they had received. They shaded the truth to gain the approval of the other church members.

In the process, however, they lost the approval of God. In fact, they lost their lives when God judged them severely for their dishonest and church-corrupting example.

Bearing false witness usually stems from our pitiful attempts at protecting our self-interest, obtaining possessions, or gaining popularity. But is it worth it? Surely if we trust God to meet our needs we'll be much better off in the end. His planning and timing are always better than ours.

EXTRA POINTS
READ JOHN 12:42-43

- Which area of concern—protection, possessions, or popularity—is most likely to tempt you to shade the truth?
- What kinds of accountability can you build into your life to help strengthen your trust in God?

ELEVEN

HUDDLE UP, GUYS!

AFTER EVERY DOWN, TEAM MEMBERS REGROUP IN THEIR HUDDLES to prepare for the next play. The offensive huddle is quite structured; the right play must be called based on down and distance to the goal line. The defensive huddle is less formal, helping players respond to what just went wrong as they anticipate the next attack.

Huddles inspire and enthuse the players as they receive new plays and strategies. Huddling brings the team together, reminds players of the other members' strengths and abilities, helps them plan, and makes sure each team member knows his part in the big picture.

Without the structure and planning in the huddle, football would deteriorate into one mob against another mob. Skill and strategy would give way to brute force.

Facing the Impossible?
We all need time in the huddle. We need time to analyze and prepare so we can return to our game and better execute our plans.

In Mark 6, Jesus huddled with His disciples. He called them together for the relational benefit of being with Him and to prepare them mentally and spiritually before sending them out into ministry. While they were in the huddle Jesus gave them their instructions.

Calling the twelve to him, he sent them out two by two and gave them authority over evil spirits.

These were His instructions: *"Take nothing for the journey except a staff—no bread, no bag, no money in your belts. Wear sandals but not an extra tunic. Whenever you enter a house, stay there until you leave that town."* (6:7-10)

The instructions were clear. The plan was in place. Now the disciples must execute that plan. And it was clear from the limited supplies that this was to be a mission of total dependence on God. Matthew 10 and Luke 9 give more detailed accounts of this same event. The disciples were directed to *preach the kingdom of God and to heal the sick.*

The first command they could obey in their own strength. They could go to the street corners and into the marketplace and proclaim the kingdom of God. What they could not do was heal the sick. They were out of their league when it came to an A-number-one, first-class miracle like making a lame man walk or a blind woman see.

Jesus had just given them a play in the huddle that they were incapable of executing. He had asked His disciples to do the impossible. If these men were anything like me, they probably came out of the huddle with great enthusiasm, charged up and ready to take on the world. But as I imagine it, about a quarter of a mile down the road the excitement began to wear off as they looked at each other and said, "What did He want us to do? We can't do that! What has He gotten us into this time?"

Forge Ahead in Faith!

In spite of their misgivings, though, the disciples did move into action. Apparently the discussion in the huddle had so inspired them that they believed Jesus and simply went forward in faith. They did what they were capable of doing on their own, preaching the kingdom of God. And they also did what took total dependence on God; they healed the sick. Then, after they had completed their assignments, they returned to the huddle.

> *The apostles gathered around Jesus and reported to him all they had done and taught. Then, because so many people were coming and going . . . they did not even have a chance to eat. . . .* (Mark 6:30-31)

What joy in fulfilling the tasks Jesus had commanded! The huddle was a victory celebration as first one and then another shared what God had done through the teaching and healing. Clearly the Lord was at work here. He had asked the disciples to do the impossible because He wanted them to depend fully on Him—and they had successfully carried out His instructions.

The reward for their faith was simple: more opportunities for service, and more impossible challenges. Before they could finish celebrating the victory, more people came to them in need of physical and spiritual assistance. Christ's team members were so busy they could hardly stop to eat.

God wants us to be about the business of trusting Him to provide the resources to do the impossible. What will your "impossible" situation be today? Loving an unlovable spouse? Supporting an ungrateful relative? Working faithfully for an unreasonable employer? Facing the death of a loved one?

Yes, God calls us to do the impossible. But He huddles with us, providing the grace and strength we need to walk each step of the way.

EXTRA POINTS
READ JOHN 15:4-5

- Which do you enjoy more: "time in the huddle" with Christ, or "executing the play" and serving Christ?
- When did it appear that God was calling you to an impossible task? How did you respond? How will you likely respond in the future?

TWELVE

WE'RE ALL TEAMMATES

I PLAYED CENTER ON OFFENSE BECAUSE I KNEW THAT WOULD BE THE only way I'd ever get to touch the football. Mom bought my school clothes from the "Husky" rack, and that doomed me to the obscurity of the interior line. But I felt there was something unique about being the center.

One big difference is that you're always a little bit slower to throw a block than everyone else, because your first responsibility is to make a clean exchange of the ball to the quarterback. This makes it easier for the defense to beat you to a pulp, hoping that at some point you'll produce a sloppy snap that results in a fumble.

Of course, if there is ever a problem and a snap is fumbled, it's always the center's fault. The quarterback—perfect as he is—could never be guilty of a thing like that. He's incapable of pulling away too soon, for instance, or of simply dropping the ball. No, the center takes the blame.

You see, quarterbacks are special and they make things happen on every play. Their athletic ability and leadership skills require them to make key decisions throughout the game. Centers just have to lift the ball a few inches . . . and wait . . . for their beating.

Maybe I wanted to be a quarterback. But I knew that playing center was as close as I would get.

Every Ability Important

It's easy for centers to envy quarterbacks. The spotlight focused on quarterbacks never hits the center—unless he makes a mistake. After the game the quarterback does an interview as the center slips away to the showers. Coaches have special meetings with quarterbacks but rarely have time for a center. Yet both players are necessary if the team is to function at all.

Just as centers can become jealous of quarterbacks, so too, those who have the gifts of serving behind the scenes in the church can begin to envy those whom God has entrusted with speaking gifts. First Peter 4:10-11 says,

> *Each one should use whatever gift he has received to serve others, faithfully administering God's grace in its various forms. If anyone speaks, he should do it as one speaking the very words of God. If anyone serves, he should do it with the strength God provides, so that in all things God may be praised through Jesus Christ. To Him be the glory and the power for ever and ever. Amen.*

We tend to honor the up-front speaking gifts over the gifts that are more functional. The preachers, teachers, missionaries, and counselors tend to get more attention and praise than the team members who change light bulbs and set up chairs for the next meeting. But without both, the church cannot function well.

The challenge before each of us is to find our gift and use

it to God's glory. If that gift happens to be a speaking gift, then we are directed to speak the very words of God. The only way to do this with certainty is to study God's Word and communicate its truth with as much skill and authority as we can develop. We don't have the option of being lazy or unproductive with our gifts. We owe it to God and we owe it to our brothers and sisters in Christ to study and communicate well.

On the other hand, if our gift is to serve others, we must rely on God's strength to apply our abilities in the most effective ways. Those who serve cannot neglect the gift they've been given. They must fill the gaps and work hard to provide a smooth-running operation in which the speaking gifts can function properly. But if we begin to compare gifts, some of us will resent the honor and attention that comes to those who speak. We will fester until the toxin of our negative attitude poisons the entire body of Christ.

For God's Glory
I loved the old TV commercial in which Dan Marino buys gloves for his offensive linemen as Christmas presents. The point is, if Marino takes care of his linemen they, in turn, will be eager to serve and take care of him.

If you have a public gift, don't take for granted those around you who are gifted for behind-the-scenes service. Be sensitive to their needs and offer the kind of appreciation that we all need from time to time.

But the purpose of all this isn't just to have a group of believers who get along well, even though that's important. The ultimate goal is to bring glory to God. The speaking gifts and the serving gifts will all bring honor to God when teammates exercise them in a spirit of love.

Without a quarterback and a center, a football team just won't work. And neither will the body of Christ function without those who are ready and willing to serve and those who are prepared and eager to speak. Find your gift and begin using it to bring glory to God today.

EXTRA POINTS
READ EPHESIANS 4:4-7, 11-13

- What specific gifts do you think God has entrusted to you? When have you seen these gifts working effectively on behalf of others?
- Think of those who use their gifts behind the scenes in your local church. How could you express encouragement and appreciation to these folks in the days ahead?

THIRTEEN

KEEP YOUR HELMET ON

OUR POP WARNER TEAM WAS RUNNING FROM ONE PRACTICE FIELD to another down a pathway that led through a wooded area of Columbia Park. We'd been coached never to remove our helmets except for designated breaks. So we looked like a trail of ants with our oversized heads and spindly bodies winding through the foliage.

The Douglas Fir trees around us were old and tall. They'd weathered many storms and their thick branches blotted out most of the sunlight overhead. But we were totally shocked when, without warning, a huge branch gave way and plummeted toward the ground, heading right at teammate Don's head. The four-inch-round limb crashed into the boy's helmet, splitting it down the middle and knocking Don into lala land.

The helmet was broken but it saved his life.

When Pain Crashes Down

Sometimes problems come crashing into our lives right out of the blue. We've been going forward, minding our own business, when without warning we get a call that death has taken a loved one, we notice an unusual lump, or the boss calls us into the office—and the news is not good. It can be anything and it can fall on our heads at the most unexpected moment.

What shall we do? One response is to ask ourselves at least three critical questions each time these limbs come falling into our world, leaving us stunned and numb. Here's the first: *Is this a discipline from God?* Hebrews 12:5-7 addresses this issue—

> *My son, do not make light of the Lord's discipline, and do not lose heart when he rebukes you, because the Lord disciplines those he loves, and he punishes everyone he accepts as a son . . . . For what son is not disciplined by his father?*

God's discipline clearly demonstrates that we are part of His family. He cares about us enough to bring correction into our lives. It isn't pleasant, but it is designed by a loving God to get our attention and to direct our thoughts and behaviors back to Him and away from danger. Once we come to our senses and repent of our sinful ways, we will appreciate living in a family that loves us enough to confront us and set us on the proper course.

The discipline God brings into our lives isn't meant to paralyze us with remorse. We need not lose heart if we find that God is redirecting us back to Himself, even if it's by means of a painful experience. Pleasure allows us the privilege of oblivion, but pain makes us think deeply about our lives. In our times of difficulty we wrestle with our inner selves. And that can produce wonderful results.

Here's the second question we can ask in a time of trial: *Could this be a test?* Job was a godly man who faced testing beyond what anyone I know has ever faced. He lost his children, his wealth, his honor, and his health. The only thing remaining was a cranky wife who tormented him all the more. Yet he passed the test, refusing to curse God and die. He learned much from his encounter with God. Job was unaware of the cosmic struggle that was underway between the Lord and Satan, but he shouldered his load with tremendous commitment to God in the midst of his pain and loss.

God must have thought very highly of Job to allow him to face such a massive testing. In 1 Corinthians 10:13 we have the promise,

And God is faithful; he will not let you be tempted beyond what you can bear.

When tough times come, realize that God highly esteems you and counts you worthy of the test.

Now for the third question to ask: *Am I simply an innocent bystander in this case?* Yes, we can get caught in the crossfire of a sinful world. There are problems of pain and death associated with sin that have implications for our world, creating traumatic situations for all of us. In Luke 13:4-5 Jesus speaks about a tragic incident in which a tower crumbled and killed eighteen people. He says,

"Those eighteen who died when the tower in Siloam fell on them—do you think they were more guilty than all the others living in Jerusalem? I tell you, no!"

His point is that bad things do happen in a world that is under sin's destructive curse. And, after all, God has allowed human beings the freedom of their wills. Much good and much pain result from human decisions.

So we must examine each limb that crashes into our lives. Is this a corrective action from a loving God? Is it a test to build us and strengthen us for the next challenge coming our way? Or is this simply an ugly reminder of human freedom and sin's temporary reign in the world?

Crises will come and they will crash in upon us when we least expect them. Don't be shocked. But do be prepared to ask yourself what it all means. Asking the Lord the right questions can help us formulate the proper response.

EXTRA POINTS
READ PSALM 64:1-10

- What painful circumstances have crashed into your life in the past year? How have you coped?
- Of the three questions to ask, which is most meaningful to you? Why?

FOURTEEN

UNDEFEATED SEASON

WHEN WE MET IN THE LOCKER ROOM BEFORE THE LAST GAME OF OUR eighth-grade season, the coach gathered us around him and began his traditional pre-game pep talk. But this time it was different—no yelling, no animation, no pounding fists. This time he spoke in quiet, almost reverent, tones. And he didn't talk long. He simply said, "You'll probably never get another chance in life to play on an undefeated championship team. Go out there and win this one. If you do, you'll have something that no one can ever take away from you for the rest of your life."

We drove from Columbia Park in North Portland, across town to Lenz Park to play under the lights. A season of kid's football and flag football had left the field a mess. It was one giant mud hole and the rain was still pouring down. Sheets and sheets of icy cold rain drenched everyone who turned out to witness the final Pop Warner contest of the year.

It was a defensive struggle, to say the least. We scored early and that ended the action. We won. We were the undefeated City Champions.

Forgetting What's Past
An unblemished record is rare at any level of football. Only the

Miami Dolphins went undefeated at 16-0 on their way to a Super Bowl victory. But an unblemished record in life is impossible. According to 1 John 1:8,

If we claim to be without sin, we deceive ourselves and the truth is not in us.

And John is writing to Christians here. We're fooling ourselves if we deny the failures in our past. But we undermine the courage we'll need to face the future if we allow past defeats to occupy our attention and dictate our self-image. The apostle Paul experienced many defeats but understood the importance of forgetting them and moving forward. In Philippians 3:13-14 he says,

Forgetting what is behind and straining toward what is ahead, I press on toward the goal to win the prize for which God has called me heavenward in Christ Jesus.

Paul wasn't expecting the Philippians to erase the memory of their former sins. But he did expect them to find freedom from the past. Forgetting means undercutting the authority those events once held over our lives and not allowing them to dictate the future. First Corinthians 6:9-10 provides a list of some of the most destructive sins that can dominate our lives,

Do you not know that the wicked will not inherit the kingdom of God? Do not be deceived: Neither the sexually immoral nor idolaters nor adulterers nor male prostitutes nor homosexual offenders nor thieves nor the greedy nor drunkards nor slanderers nor swindlers will inherit the kingdom of God.

We all struggle with something on such biblical lists, but the point is not who is being *excluded* from God's kingdom; the point is that these are the people whose lives have been changed and who now populate God's kingdom. The passage goes on,

> *And that is what some of you were. But you were washed, you were sanctified, you were justified in the name of the Lord Jesus Christ and by the Spirit of our God.* (Verse 11)

Starting Over

In John 8 a bloodthirsty mob confronted Jesus with a woman caught in the act of adultery. The man had disappeared, but the woman was facing death by stoning as punishment for her transgression. Jesus calmed the situation, confronted the people with their own hypocrisy, and dispersed the crowd. Then, when the throng dwindled, Jesus addressed the woman. He left her with these words, "Go now and leave your sinful life."

Saved from the jagged stones and crushing blows of the mob's hateful, hypocritical words, she stood at a crossroads. One path led back to a life that sought satisfaction through momentary pleasure and independence from God. The other path led to restoration and the fulfillment of pleasing God from a pure heart. The first route would end with a losing season, the second would begin and end with an unblemished record before God.

Christ's offer is the same for us today. We can continue in our various forms of rebellion or we can accept His forgiveness and start fresh, undefeated. We will never attain a life free from sin this side of heaven. In the Lord's eyes, however, we are perfect and pure as we accept His forgiveness and cleansing.

EXTRA POINTS
READ HEBREWS 10:19-23

- In what way is a sin of the past holding you back or dictating your future?
- How can you show your appreciation to God for wiping the losses out of your win/loss record?

FIFTEEN

That Little Piece of Plastic

LIKE ANCIENT ARMIES FACING OFF ON THE FIELD OF BATTLE, THE two teams line up and stare at each other, looks of grim determination hardening the combatant's faces, their muscles tensing just before the blast of the whistle—football's bugle call to commence the charge. The crowds have cheered, the bands have played, and now in the hush just before the engagement, it is time to focus all concentration on the opponent.

What can match the excitement of the opening kickoff? As a kid sitting in the stands I was captivated by kickoffs, my adrenaline surging as if I were actually in the game.

My Job: The Tee

Two years before I was old enough to play Pop Warner football, I'd volunteered to be equipment manager for the mighty St. John's Optimists, my older brother's team. My duties included being entrusted with the kicking tee on game days.

When the whistle blew to end the kickoff, my job was to run onto the field and retrieve the tee. But almost without exception, the excitement would overwhelm me, and I would forget my assignment. The coach would yell at me and I would have to race onto the field in front of both teams, their parents, and everyone else in the stands to get that little piece of plastic back to safety. My forgetfulness was on display for everyone to see.

Too Easy to Forget

This didn't happen just once or twice. It happened on almost every kickoff. Time and time again I'd play the buffoon. No matter how hard I'd try to remember and determine to get the tee, during the kickoff excitement I would forget my commitment and fail to fulfill my obligation.

Forgetfulness happens in our spiritual journeys as well. Time and time again God pours blessings into our lives. We rejoice for a while and then our memories of His grace and goodness begin to fade. Here's how Psalm 78 puts it:

> *He decreed statutes for Jacob and established the law in Israel, which he commanded our forefathers to teach their children, so the next generation would know them, even the children yet to be born, and they in turn would tell their children. Then they would put their trust in God and would not forget his deeds but would keep his commands.* (Verses 5-7)

Without the benefit of a history of God's protection and provision, each generation enters the world unaware of how God provided in the past. If we forget what God has done for us, we will never be able to transfer this knowledge to our children. But more importantly, we will erode the impact these memories have on our own ongoing walk with God.

We must recall how God provided peace in times of stress and turmoil—the check that came in the mail when the cupboard was bare, the broken relationship that was restored, or the job that came out of the blue. All too often these past blessings grow dim in the red-hot turmoil of today's trouble.

My forgetfulness with the kicking tee happened when I became engrossed in the excitement around me and failed to focus on my appointed task. We too can become distracted by life's many pressing activities and lose sight of God's past faithfulness. At the first hint of problems our memories seem to go blank. Has it happened to you?

Yet we can count on God to help with our current problem because He has demonstrated His love in the past, and He does not change. Hebrews 13:8 says,

Jesus Christ is the same yesterday and today and forever.

We can count on God's help in the future with confidence as we remember His unchanging love for us in the past. Don't let the busyness of today, or the excitement of the moment, rob you of powerful recollections of God's unfailing love. Retrieve those memories every time you enter another daily battle.

EXTRA POINTS
READ 2 PETER 1:10-15

- What things could you do to keep God's acts of love and mercy at the forefront of your thinking?
- Is there something in your life that you can change in order to allow more time to meditate on God's past goodness toward you? What first step could you take?

SIXTEEN

HURT OR INJURED?

MY RIGHT ARM WOULDN'T WORK. I COULD FEEL A STRANGE PAIN tingling from my shoulder down to my little finger and I couldn't move my arm or make the burning sensation subside.

There had been a pile-up near the goal line, and I was at the bottom. Someone, no telling if he was friend or foe, had stepped on my elbow. The cleat had struck my "funny bone," causing me to lumber off the field with my right hand supporting my left arm.

"What's the matter with you?" bellowed my coach as he charged toward me. As a tenth-grader I was already intimidated by my crusty old coach, but at this moment I was terrified of him.

"My arm," I managed. "It's hurt."

"Hurt?" he hollered back. "My ballplayers play hurt. Get in there, Johnson," he yelled, and an equally terrified substitute ran onto the field. Then the coach turned to one of the assistants and said, "Find out if Bolin is hurt or injured."

Time for Healing

Hurt or injured? I had never considered the difference, but I was about to find out. We were expected to play with some level of discomfort. Football is, after all, a contact sport. Bruises, cuts, strains, and sore muscles are natural and expected. But injuries are different. They are the significant wounds that take time to heal and need special attention. These are the breaks and tears that put us in street clothes on the sidelines. We play through the bumps and bruises but we must heal from the injuries before we are capable of once again entering the arena and participating fully.

In the Christian life we become injured by the brutal attacks of others or by our own willful disobedience. The destructive results of our sinful behavior can produce crippling effects in our lives. In a moment of weakness we can injure ourselves and be carried off the field of play. When that happens we must find a place of recovery. We must step back and rehabilitate ourselves if we hope to ever rejoin the team and return to the game.

Scripture provides an example of the rehab process that took place in the life of King David. He was injured when he sinned with Bathsheba, having been overcome by lust and taking another man's wife. To cover his sin he hatched a plot that ended with the murder of a faithful friend. By his sin, David injured himself and others deeply, and as he reflected on his predicament he wrote these words in Psalm 51:1 —

Have mercy on me, O God,
    according to your unfailing love;
according to your great compassion
    blot out my transgressions.

David's road to recovery began with acknowledging his sin,

remembering God's character, and requesting forgiveness. He was in obvious pain and on the spiritual sidelines when he turned to God in order to start back on the road to wholeness.

David was eager to return to front-line action, but he knew that his wounds had put the spotlight on his shortcomings. He needed to deal with the cause of his problem to avoid re-injuring himself with the same sin in the future. He goes on to say,

> *Create in me a pure heart, O God,*
> *and renew a steadfast spirit within me.* (Verse 10)

A pure heart and steadfast spirit would be the protection he needed to avoid another crushing injury similar to the one from which he was recovering. Without this defense he would be vulnerable to sin and could wind up back on the sidelines.

The One Who Heals

David captures the essence of God's desire to provide healing and forgiveness to those who truly want to return to active participation. In verses 16-17 he says,

> *You do not delight in sacrifice, or I would bring it;*
> *you do not take pleasure in burnt offerings.*
> *The sacrifices of God are a broken spirit;*
> *a broken and contrite heart,*
> *O God, you will not despise.*

David realized that God isn't eager for one more religious event or ceremony. What God wants is the love and commitment of a broken heart that has found restoration in His compassionate forgiveness.

The brokenness of our lives is the starting point for recovery. Until we realize the severity of our sinful injury we will struggle through life playing with pain, never capable of high-quality performance, unwilling to receive assistance and healing.

Each of the three verses mentioned has a common thread— "O God." That's significant because there is no forgiveness, no purity of heart, and no true restoration of relationship apart from "O God." Our healing may be assisted by pastors, counselors, and Christian friends, but those folks are only instruments who can never substitute for the Healer Himself. He is the One who specializes in restoring our broken hearts.

EXTRA POINTS
READ PSALM 69:29-34

- Would you say the painful parts of your life are due to hurts or due to injuries?
- How do you typically react when you're hurt or injured? How would you *like* to respond in the future?

SEVENTEEN

JUST GETTING DIRTY?

I WAS ON THE TEAM, BUT I DIDN'T GET TO PLAY MUCH DURING MY high school football days. My jersey was covered with mud and my arms were bruised during the week, but on Friday nights I mainly sat on the bench in my nice, clean uniform.

I didn't mind sitting that much—until the end of the game. At that point we had to leave the field and walk past the crowd to the locker room. The real players were covered with mud and grass stains. Head-on collisions had streaked their helmets with the opponents' colors. Mixed in with the filth and grime were some of us still wearing sparkling clean uniforms.

To remedy the problem, several of us "clean jersey guys" devised a plan to get as dirty as possible during the pre-game warm-ups. We'd find the muddiest spot to do calisthenics. Falling down as often as possible, we'd make sure our jerseys were encrusted with dirt like the other guys'. Ultimate victory meant getting some sod to hang from our face masks.

When we did get in the game for kickoffs or extra points, we'd look for a muddy spot and try to block an opponent who happened to be in that area. In other words, playing the game would have been nice, but we were much more concerned with looking the part.

Beyond Image Management

Many of us Christians don't mind participating in areas of service and spiritual exercise, but we are mainly interested in looking the part. I am often more concerned with what friends and associates think of me than with God's evaluation of my performance. In Colossians 1:10-12 we read a segment of Paul's prayer for the Colossian Christians:

And we pray this in order that you may live a life worthy of the Lord and may please him in every way: bearing fruit in every good work, growing in the knowledge of God, being strengthened with all power . . . and joyfully giving thanks to the Father.

God wants us to be legitimate players who are worthy of membership on His team. He knows all and sees all, and there is no way to fool Him into thinking we are genuine spiritually if all we do is go through the motions and present an image of participation while just sitting on the end of the bench.

What does it mean to please God? How do we put a smile on His face and make Him proud of us? I find four answers in these verses.

First, we can bear fruit in every good work. Fruit means results and in the New Testament, fruit can refer to the result of new converts or the result of Christlike character. Either or both could be in mind in this passage. A true team member shows internal and external results because of what Christ has done in his life.

Second, we must be increasing in the knowledge of God. To be a true participant we must be learning more and more about our Lord. And what could substitute for God's Word when it comes to increasing our knowledge of Him? To be a real player we must be reading, studying, and contemplating the eternal truths on a regular basis.

Third, we are to be strengthened with all power. Strength doesn't happen after one visit to the weight room. We gain power through repetitions. The more we exercise trust in God and serve Him, the more we gain confidence and power to accomplish bigger and more challenging tasks for Him. There is no substitute for consistent discipline in our spiritual lives. Practice, practice, and more practice prepares us for the tasks ahead.

Fourth, we are to joyfully give thanks to the Father. When all is said and done, it is the Father's love for us that allows us to participate at all. Without His provision there is no team and we are not players. He alone is worthy of our thanks. Thinking about that should produce nothing but joy.

When we play the game of image management, we fail to work toward godly character development. If image management dominates our lives, we are no better than the "clean jersey guys" who rolled in the mud. We might get a little dirty, but we miss all the rewards of truly participating in the game.

EXTRA POINTS
READ EPHESIANS 1:15-21

- Have you ever done something to manage your image before people that ended up damaging your character before God? What happened? What did you learn?
- What things are you doing to strengthen your character these days?

EIGHTEEN

YOU'RE ON THE SPECIAL TEAM

MOST OF MY HIGH SCHOOL PLAYING TIME WAS LIMITED TO KICKOFFS, extra points, punts, and if we got way ahead or way behind I might see some regular action near the end of the game. Most of the starters played on either offense or defense, while a few truly exceptional team members were on both offense *and* defense, á la Deion Sanders.

But none of the starters wanted to play on kickoffs, punts, and extra points. The players with these assignments are referred to as "Special Teams." In high school we were called the "Nut Squad." And we felt anything but special. The truly special players were the ones with dirt on their jerseys at the end of the game.

Why So Special?

As Christians, each of us is a member of God's "special team." And there are at least three reasons why we are special. First, we're special because God created us. Psalm 139:13-14 says,

> *You created my inmost being; you knit me together in my mother's womb. I praise you because I am fearfully and wonderfully made; your works are wonderful, I know that full well.*

These verses marvel over the process of conception, development, and birth. But God's creation of a life involves much more than the color of eyes and the length of feet. Our creation has to do with personality and thought process, likes and dislikes, expression and will. Thus our uniqueness makes us special. I may wish that my nose was less special, or that my ears were less like sails on a boat, but the combination of characteristics God has given to you and me—these make us special.

Second, we have a place on God's "special team" because of our salvation. Jesus demonstrated our specialness to Him by willingly bearing the punishment we deserved. In the Garden of Gethsemane He prayed to the Father to provide a way around the horrible agony that awaited Him, but finding no acceptable alternative He willingly paid the terrible price. He gave His life, not because we were special, but rather to *make us* special.

More amazing to me—as a dad who lost a child to leukemia—is that God the Father allowed His Son to die in my place. I would have done anything to save my daughter's life and certainly wouldn't have allowed her to die if I could have intervened. Yet God the Father chose to give His Son in exchange for me, even though He had options that were unavailable to me. In Matthew 26:53-54 Jesus speaks to His disciples in the midst of His arrest and says,

> *"Do you think I cannot call on my Father, and he will at once put at my disposal more than twelve legions of angels? But how then would the Scriptures be fulfilled that say it must happen in this way?"*

Jesus died willingly in my place and God the Father stood by and watched. Not because He lacked love for His Son but because He had such a love for me. He chose to love me and that choice made me special.

Besides our creation and salvation, which qualify us to be on God's "special team," we receive a third unique gift that enhances our specialness. According to 1 Corinthians 12:4-6,

There are different kinds of gifts, but the same Spirit.
There are different kinds of service, but the same Lord.
There are different kinds of working, but the same God
works all of them in all men.

Membership on God's "special team" equips us with the abilities to fulfill our unique role within the body. God provides everything we need to be in His kingdom.

We must never lose the perspective that God has designated us for His "special team," and that it has nothing to do with how much money we have, what kind of car we drive, or how much education we have received. We are special because God created us, died for us, and equipped us for every kind of assignment He might call us to carry out.

EXTRA POINTS
READ EPHESIANS 5:1-2

- What is special about your personality or competencies? What things about you might God use in a special way?
- How does reflecting upon the Father's act of giving His Son affect your view of Him? Your view of yourself?

NINETEEN

The Vicious, Blind-Side Attack

I FELT COCKY AND CONFIDENT MOVING UP FROM THE SECOND STRING to play with the first-team varsity. I knew it would only be until the real starter's injury healed, but it felt good to be included with the best our team had to offer. During this particular practice, the junior varsity team (made up exclusively of sophomores) had been coached to resemble the offense of next Friday night's opponent. We were preparing for a full scrimmage.

As a junior I was thrilled to be a part of the mainly senior first team and thought I'd make the most of my two-day promotion. After the coach admonished us not to tackle the quarterback, we lined up over the ball.

I was the left defensive tackle and my job was to get into the backfield and create as much havoc as possible. So I did! When the ball moved, I charged ahead into the gap between the center and the guard. *These guys are worse than I expected,* I thought, as I met almost no resistance. Right before my eyes the quarterback put the ball into the stomach of the running back. He lowered his head and came directly toward me. I could already hear the coach praising my skill and hard work. My first play at left tackle and I'm already a star. . . .

While preparing to receive the accolades of the coaches

81

and the praise of my teammates, I caught something of interest just to my right. Without losing sight of the ball carrier, I turned enough to catch a glimpse of a pulling guard just before he knocked me half way into the next county.

Yes, I'd reached the backfield with ease, but I'd been suckered into a trap play to make me ineffective. I fell for the deception and paid the price.

Confronting the Lies

Life is full of deception. We feel great about ourselves and our situation in life, and about that time, out of the corner of our eye, we see trouble heading our way.

Because the apostle Paul had a deep concern for the church at Corinth, he wrote at least two letters and visited those believers in order to help them through some deceptions.

He did it by challenging the authority and message of certain false prophets who preached a different Jesus, a different Spirit, and a different gospel than Paul's true message from God. Of these men Paul says in 2 Corinthians 11:13:

For such men are false apostles, deceitful workmen, masquerading as apostles of Christ. And no wonder, for Satan himself masquerades as an angel of light.

The pulling guards of this life would love to knock us off our feet, inflicting pain, and putting us on the sidelines. During a tense confrontation, Jesus spoke very directly to His own adversaries:

"You belong to your father, the devil, and you want to carry out your father's desire. He was a murderer from the

beginning, not holding to the truth, for there is no truth in him. When he lies, he speaks his native language, for he is a liar and the father of lies." (John 8:44)

Satan apparently knows that the best way to tell a lie is to make it appear as much like the truth as possible. Lies are easy to spot when they're ugly and repulsive, but when they look good, and appear even better than the real thing, they are very difficult to distinguish from the truth.

There are lies about ourselves: "I am better than Joe" or, "I am worse than Bill." There are lies about our loved ones: "My life would be better if I had married Peggy Sue." There are lies about God: "He won't mind if I sin just a little; after all, He knows I'm only human." Such lies are just close enough to the truth to make them seem plausible. But they are far enough away to set us up for a devastating hit.

The best way to defend yourself against a pulling guard is to know your assignment, know the plans of the enemy, and carry out your task while staying vigilant in protecting yourself. When you sense the onslaught coming on, it's best to confront the pulling guard head on. And when you realize a lie is targeting your life, defend yourself from a blind-side attack. Turn and face it with the truth of God's Word.

EXTRA POINTS
READ 2 CORINTHIANS 4:1-5

- Have you ever discovered that you were choosing to believe a lie? What did you do?
- What half-truth might be distorting your view of God at present?

TWENTY

PASS BLOCKING

THE QUARTERBACK DROPS BACK FOR A PASS WITH FIVE QUICK crossover steps. He hurriedly surveys the situation down field. Looks left. Looks right. Looks left again. Time is running out. In just a few seconds more he'll be a sitting duck for marauding pass-rushers hoping to bury him where he stands.

Who will protect this vulnerable skill-player from a bone-rattling hit?

The offensive linemen. Guarding the quarterback is the supreme goal of these hulking sentries whose names are never mentioned unless there's a penalty flag on the ground near their feet—or they're being carried off the field on a stretcher.

The quarterback's health is the standard by which these men will be judged, play after play. And when the quarterback drops back to pass, the stakes are high, the danger great, the potential risks and rewards definitely multiplied.

Protection Needed

A successful pass often means the difference between victory and defeat. It all depends on the ones offering crucial protection. But what about protecting a successful life? Scripture tells us to guard at least four things if we are to achieve that. First, Proverbs 22:5 says,

In the paths of the wicked lie thorns and snares,
but he who guards his soul stays far from them.

Our souls are eternally valuable and must be protected.
Thorns and snares picture the temptations and problems we
experience while walking along life's pathway. Guarding our
souls begins by choosing pathways that lead away from temptations that entangle us and leave us ineffective. We must rely
upon the security of walking closely with God and moving
away from danger.

Where are you walking? Is the trail lined with danger and
potential pain? Even more importantly, are you headed in a
direction of safety and security? Spiritually, we walk with our
eyes. So if we are to guard our souls, we must protect our eyes.
Television, movies, the Internet, even the check-out line at the
grocery store can all be places of snares and thorns. Walking
recklessly down dangerous pathways will lead to pain and
failure.

In addition to guarding our souls, we must guard the
gospel. As the apostle Paul challenged his young mentor
Timothy:

Guard the good deposit that was entrusted to you—guard
it with the help of the Holy Spirit who lives in us.
(2 Timothy 1:14)

I take the good deposit to mean the gospel that Timothy
was to share with his parishioners in the church of Ephesus.
The clear presentation of the gospel was to be the priority in his
life, and he was to guard the good news by keeping it pure and

free from error. I have little problem maintaining an orthodox view, but I struggle with keeping evangelism a priority in my daily life. Perhaps we need to do a better job of being aware of the seekers all around us. In the case of the gospel, to guard it is to give it away.

Our third protective task is to guard our friendships. Peter writes,

Be on your guard so that you may not be carried away by the error of lawless men . . . (2 Peter 3:17)

We're called to guard against acquaintances who could influence our lives toward lawlessness. As Christians we're challenged to build relationships with those who need the love and truth of Christ. However, we must shun the negative influences attached to these relationships. While trying to lift others up we risk being dragged down. Our noble intentions may be commendable, but the dangers of adapting to the world's standards are real. Stay on guard against relationships that will influence you in the wrong directions. The people who influence our lives can be our greatest allies or our worst enemies.

The apostle John's last words in 1 John were,

Little children, guard yourselves from idols. (1 John 5:21, NASB)

Here we have the fourth area needing protection: God's authority in our lives. We typically think of idols as being statues of wood and stone. In reality, an idol is anything that takes over God's rightful place as Lord of our lives. These idols may be obviously evil, such as drugs, illicit sex, greed, or some other destructive agent controlling our lives. But often God is displaced by good things gone out of control: a job, a relationship, a hobby, or a good cause. We must guard our lives against anything that takes the attention and focus away from God.

Guarding our souls, the gospel, our friendships, and God's authority leads to successful living. Give serious attention to protecting these critical components of your life. Don't allow any form of attack to sack you for a loss.

EXTRA POINTS
READ PSALM 25:15-22

- What kinds of temptations require your utmost vigilance? What helps you the most in this struggle?
- What idols seem to threaten God's place of authority in your life? Why are these things often so attractive?

TWENTY-ONE

PLAYER TRADES

Trading players has always been a part of professional football. For years the arguments have raged regarding who came out ahead when one star was traded for another. *Hershel Walker traded from Dallas to Minnesota for so many players?*

Every general manager makes trades to improve his team, but injuries, team chemistry, and the toll of previous seasons create some surprise winners and some unexpected losers.

What's the Value?

To trade or not to trade, that is the question. Judging the value of players is a challenge, but some trades are no-brainers. Easy to see are the lopsided trades that should never occur. No team would trade a great, young quarterback for a twelve-year veteran lineman. The quarterback position is valuable, as is the prospect of a full career compared to one or two more seasons. This trade should never happen; in fact, this trade shouldn't even be considered.

But we do make that trade all too often. That is, we trade our most valuable possession for things that have little or no value and satisfy but for a moment. In Matthew 16:26 Jesus asks two penetrating questions in this regard:

"What good will it be for a man if he gains the whole world, yet forfeits his soul? Or what can a man give in exchange for his soul?"

How Long?

The first question deals with the issue of *length of impact*. Most football trades have short-term and long-term implications. What might be great for this season may require giving up a potential all-star for years to come. When we trade our souls we face the same dilemma. The short term payoff appears attractive, but the long term results are terribly destructive. A short-term affair brings long-term ruin. A harsh word spoken in an instant of anger can never be recaptured. An impulsive decision may create confusion and pain down through the years.

The challenge of Jesus' question, then, is to consider whether the trades we're making will provide success in this life or in eternity. Will our trades help us this season but jeopardize the future? The pressures of the world focus our attention on short-term successes while Jesus asks the haunting question, "How long will it last?"

We are always trading the days and moments God has given us for something. Is it something of eternal value? Are we trading our time, energy, and talents for things that will last beyond earthly existence?

How Good?

The second question deals with *relative quality*. What can a man give in exchange for his soul? Is there anything worthy of consideration when your soul is at stake?

We move through life responding to our needs while rarely reflecting on the true value of what we are giving up compared with what we receive. What are we giving up when we justify saving a few dollars by fudging on our tax deductions? What happens to our trade value when a family member receives the pain of our angry words? What is the real value of a moment of pleasure that wrecks the lives of those around us and haunts us for a lifetime?

Unfortunately, we tend to spend more time evaluating the trades made between the owners of professional football franchises than we spend evaluating the trades we make every moment of every day—the ones that impact our souls.

We need to trade the things of time for the things of eternity. The attention given to football trades is proportional to the value of the players involved. If we fail to comprehend the true value of our souls, we're likely to make a trade that receives a price well below its actual worth. God established the value of our souls when He sent His Son to die in our place, when He traded His life for ours. Recognize the value of your soul and evaluate your trades, every day, in light of its eternal worth.

EXTRA POINTS
READ ROMANS 8:18

- When have you made a bad trade?
- What is the best long-term trade you have recently made with your life? What advice would you give to others seeking such trades?

TWENTY-TWO

MAKE TIME FOR HALF TIME

Symmetry is woven into every aspect of football: eleven players per side, a mid-field stripe dividing the field in half, two end zones, two goal posts, four quarters. . . .

But there is only one half time.

Half time is my wife's favorite part of any football game, but she can't understand why TV announcers review the first half, show highlights of other games, and predict what will happen in the second half. They could be showing us marching bands and baton twirlers.

For many, the pomp and pageantry of half time is simply an entertaining diversion. But for the players and coaches, it's a critically important part of the game. Players catch their breath and regain their strength. Coaches make adjustments in the game plan, modifying their offensive and defensive strategies to counter their opponent. half time also gives the players a chance to evaluate their personal performance and dedicate themselves to improving in the second half.

Take Some Time Out . . .

We all need half times in our lives. We need the times of stepping away from the intensity and urgency of life to catch our

91

breath, adjust our strategy, and renew our commitment. In our spiritual lives, catching our breath requires time away from the draining demands of life's routines. Jesus' disciples returned from an extended ministry trip bringing back wonderful reports of God's work. But they also came back exhausted. In Mark 6:31, Jesus says to them,

> *"Come with me by yourselves to a quiet place and get some rest."*

Here we find at least three things required to enjoy the rest Jesus offers. *Come with me*—Catching our spiritual and emotional breath means including Jesus in our lives by focusing on Him and enjoying His presence as we reflect on His goodness. *By yourselves*—We must leave the distractions at home: TV, radio, newspapers, phones, and even people. These must be set aside so we can regain the spiritual strength that comes from time alone with God. *To a quiet place*—A quiet, undisturbed rendezvous point for meeting with God is essential. It might be a room in your home, a walkway through your neighborhood, a retreat site, park, or church building. Find a place where you can meet with God free of distractions and interruptions.

It's tough to make strategic adjustments in our lives while we're swamped with work, when deadlines are closing in upon us, or when our schedule overflows with appointments from early morning through the late-night hours. When the pressures build, we will find ourselves overwhelmed by the challenges before us and the battles raging on every side. But we need to establish half times to reflect on our changing world and our changing lives so that we can respond with appropriate adjustments.

. . . And Re-Commit to the Task

In Mark 3:13-14 Jesus created a half time experience for twelve very busy men who were about to adjust their life strategies.

Jesus went up on a mountainside and called to him those he wanted, and they came to him. He appointed twelve—designating them apostles—that they might be with him and that he might send them out to preach.

This half time experience marked these men for the rest of their lives. They were ordinary men with ordinary occupations. They came from various backgrounds but each was willing to let go of the past to attain something better. The strategy involves two parts: first developing a relationship with Christ; second, serving Him. Taking time for evaluation and adjustment requires assessing how well we are doing in both of these crucial areas.

First and foremost He calls us to be with Him. Are we spending time with Him and His Word? Second, we need to serve Him. Should we make any half time adjustments in our schedules or in our attitudes that will allow us to serve God more effectively?

The key emphasis of half time is the emotional recommitment to the task ahead. Are we willing to pay the price required to achieve the desired victory? After the Last Supper, Jesus took His disciples to the Garden of Gethsemane to spend the final half time of His earthly life in prayer. Kneeling before the Father He prays,

"Father . . . take this cup from me. Yet not what I will, but what you will." (Mark 14:36)

He knew the horrible price that would soon be required. Avoiding the pain and shame of the coming hours was very tempting, but He was willing to recommit Himself to providing salvation for all.

We too must take time to consider the price required to follow Christ the way He followed His Father. Let us regularly make half time recommitments to the Lord by taking time to recuperate, setting aside time to adjust our life strategy to do the things God calls us to do.

EXTRA POINTS
READ PSALM 77:11-13

- What does having "good times alone with God" mean for you? Have you had any of these times in the past weeks and months?
- What adjustments could you make in order to better serve God?

TWENTY-THREE

WHAT A COMEBACK!

I LIVE IN TYLER, TEXAS, AND I ADMIT I'M BIASED. BUT I THINK THE greatest high school football game of all time was played in November 1995, when the John Tyler Lions defeated the Plano Wildcats in a semi-final state championship game.

Let me set the scene. John Tyler was leading 41 to 17 with less than three minutes remaining in the fourth quarter. That's when Plano began its scoring barrage. First they scored a touchdown and successfully executed an on-side kick. Then they did it again and again, finally going ahead 44 to 41 with eleven seconds left to play.

Texas Stadium was rocking, with thousands of fans hollering their heads off. Plano, a suburb of Dallas, provided most of the fans, and they were going wild. Then came the final kickoff. Plano kicked deep and Roderick Dunn fielded the ball on the three-yard line. He headed up the middle of the field. He cut left. He zigged and he zagged. And he avoided every Plano defender, including the kicker, to race 97 yards for the touchdown as time ran out.

John Tyler, 48. Plano, 44.

A wild finish to a wild game.

Not Over . . . 'Til It's Over

What really matters isn't the half time score, or the score at the end of the third quarter, or the score with eleven seconds left on the clock. The final score is the only one that goes in the record book.

Come-from-behind victories make great football stories. God specializes in come-from-behind victories. Consider an amazing case in point: the story of Manasseh, King of Judah. He became king at age twelve and apparently the power and honor went to his head, for he quickly fell into gross sin.

The list of his sins and the story of his life are found in 2 Chronicles 33. He directed his worship toward Baal, the god of the Canaanites, dabbling in astrology as well. He even went so far as to build altars to pagan deities within the holy temple in Jerusalem! Under Manasseh's reign the nation sank to such a low point that the people were practicing human sacrifice. Manasseh sent his own son to this hideous, fiery death. His list of personal evils goes on to include sorcery, divination, witchcraft, and consultation with mediums and spiritists.

The Scriptures paint a pretty bleak picture of this king's personal life, but he is also condemned for how he used his position of authority as the nation's leader. Verses 9-10 state,

> *Manasseh led Judah and the people of Jerusalem astray, so that they did more evil than the nations the LORD had destroyed before the Israelites. The LORD spoke to Manasseh and his people, but they paid no attention.*

With his personal life in shambles and his public influence leading the nation into total rebellion, the Lord took drastic measures. The Assyrian army came against Jerusalem, ransacking the city and capturing the king. There were no Geneva War Crimes treaties and no Red Cross inspectors to monitor the conditions of prisoners of war. To keep Manasseh in line the Assyrians put a hook in his nose, shackled him, and took him to Babylon in total humiliation.

But while there, Manasseh came to his senses.

In his distress he sought the favor of the LORD his God and humbled himself greatly before the God of his fathers. And when he prayed to him, the LORD was moved by his entreaty and listened to his plea; so he brought him back to Jerusalem and to his kingdom. Then Manasseh knew that the LORD is God. (Verses 12-13)

This great come-from-behind victory stemmed from humility, repentance, and the unflagging mercy of God.

So Never Give Up

I hope you've avoided many of the evils that dominated Manasseh's life. But we all rebel and commit sins that alienate us from God and torment our lives. Realizing that Manasseh's sins were forgivable and that God was eager to rebuild this man's life is a great encouragement to me. God's purpose in discipline is not to exact judgment but to bring us to repentance.

Restoration began when Manasseh humbled himself. He had been humbled when his kingdom was taken from him and while he was dragged off to Babylon by the nose. But circumstances alone cannot humble our hearts. Not until Manasseh chose to humble himself did God respond. Yet, even though

Manasseh, with a forgiven heart, was restored to the throne of Judah, he lived the rest of his life with painful memories and emotional scars.

The reason come-from-behind victories are so stunning is not only because of the intense drama as the action unfolds, but because such victories are so rare. We must never expect that we will score the last touchdown as time runs out or kick the game-winning field goal for the last play. As any coach knows, it's best to go ahead early and keep extending the lead.

However, if you find yourself behind, don't hang your head in defeat. Rather, humble yourself before God, never giving up on yourself or on those you love. With the Lord, there is always hope for a great come-from-behind triumph.

EXTRA POINTS
READ EPHESIANS 2:12-13

- Think of a hopeless situation in your world—something that needs a come-from-behind victory. How willing are you to pray about this today?
- What things could you adjust in your life—rather than hoping for a last-minute comeback?

TWENTY-FOUR

TICK, TICK, TICKING AWAY . . .

THE CROWD WAS GROWING RESTLESS.

On with the game! Play ball!

Cheerleaders began to excite the crowd, heightening the anticipation. But still neither team moved.

A little man wearing a bright red sports coat stood on the 20-yard line. At the other end of the field stood both teams, ready to rejoin the fray. The officials were in place, waiting patiently. One striped shirt stood directly over the ball. The game would not continue until he moved out of the way and blew his whistle.

Let's get on with the action!

Finally, the man in the red jacket extended his right hand toward the official standing over the ball, pointed his finger into the air, twirled it three times. Then he coiled the cord that trailed from his headset and stepped off the playing field.

Yes! Go Team!

One man in a bright red coat. He controlled the players, the officials, the coaches, and the people in the stands. What made this man so powerful? Why did he alone determine the progress of the game?

It's simple: he was the TV Time-Out Man.

Timing for Everything

You see, the length of TV commercials doesn't always match the time available after punts, touchdowns, and fumble recoveries. The game can't begin until the wheels of commerce have turned, and the TV audience isn't very forgiving if a commercial runs into the start of play. Hence the little man in the red coat.

There is a time to play football and a time to sell products. We, too, have time segments in our lives; they determine how we spend our waking hours. Ecclesiastes 3:4-7 lists pairs of things that fill our lives. The list includes:

A time to weep and a time to laugh, a time to mourn and a time to dance, a time to scatter stones and a time to gather them, a time to embrace and a time to refrain, a time to search and a time to give up, a time to keep and a time to throw away, . . . a time to be silent and a time to speak.

Every experience in life has its appropriate time, but knowing how to arrange them takes wisdom and insight. It's a constant question for all of us: What should we do and when should we do it?

Matching God's Timing

Ecclesiastes 3:11 offers some clues about how to order our lives:

He has made everything beautiful in its time. He has also set eternity in the hearts of men; yet they cannot fathom what God has done from beginning to end.

God has made everything beautiful in its time. The time of silence or of the spoken word are both appropriate if we are sensitive to the moment and follow God's leading. Yet few formulas will apply to every situation in life; therefore, matching our timing with God's timing is essential.

God expects us to be good stewards of time, that valuable and fleeting commodity we all possess in equal amounts during each moment. However, the real challenge is to understand the eternity that God has placed in our hearts.

Eternity and infinity are different though similar. The best way I have found to catch a glimpse of eternity is to gaze into the stars on a clear night. Whether or not I am looking into "forever," I get a feeling of infinity. I sense that something is going on forever. Eternity is in my heart and I too will go on forever.

Not only will my life go on, but each and every person on earth has eternity in his heart. That makes the issue of time all the more important. Am I using my time allotment appropriately to make a difference for eternity? Will others enjoy eternity with God because of my time usage? Or will I fiddle away the opportunities God has provided me?

As our time ticks away every day, we are called to balance the contemplation of God's good will with the accomplishment of His good works. Sometimes I need the little man in the red jacket to look me in the eye and say, "Hey! It's time to get the game going again. Play ball."

EXTRA POINTS
READ GALATIANS 6:7-10 AND ECCLESIASTES 3:1-8

- What would it mean for you to use time more wisely?
- How can you tell when you have a balance in your life in light of the advice in Ecclesiastes 3?

TWENTY-FIVE

JUST LEAVE SOME SHREDS

A FISTFUL OF THREADS . . . AND THE BALL-CARRIER LONG GONE.

How could you defend against it? This new wrinkle created by the offense was too much for the defensive coaches. They scratched their heads and stayed up late, but this time the offensive strategists had out-maneuvered them, and there was nothing they could do about it.

The new weapon was the tear-away jersey. In college football during the late sixties and early seventies a ball handler could wear a jersey made of cloth designed to rip into pieces when a defender grabbed hold. Instead of dragging down the running back with a vice-like grasp of shirt tail, the would-be tackler found himself with nothing in hand but a few shreds of cotton.

Hi, There!

Eventually tear-away jerseys were outlawed, bringing greater parity to both sides of the line of scrimmage. At least it lowered the cost of equipment for those who ruined several jerseys per game!

Escaping the clutches of the enemy is no new challenge, of course. We all face temptations that grab at us and try to pull us down. Perhaps we would do well to put on a tear-away jersey when we sense temptations reaching in our direction. In Genesis 39 we find the story of Joseph encountering a temptation that often drags down men and women—sexual immorality.

The temptation came from his boss' wife. This wasn't the first time she'd come on to him, but this time the circumstances made him more vulnerable.

> *Now Joseph was well-built and handsome, and after a while his master's wife took notice of Joseph and said, "Come to bed with me!" But he refused. "With me in charge," he told her, "my master does not concern himself with anything in the house; everything he owns he has entrusted to my care. . . . How then could I do such a wicked thing and sin against God?" . . .*
>
> *One day he went into the house to attend to his duties, and none of the household servants was inside. She caught him by his cloak and said, "Come to bed with me!" But he left his cloak in her hand and ran out of the house.*
> (Verses 6-12)

Joseph was no different from you or me. He was in his late teens or early twenties with hyperactive hormones. Yet he wasn't looking for an opportunity to sin; it came after him. In spite of the enticing come-on, Joseph was committed to two great perspectives and he took one decisive action. These allowed him to tear free of the temptation without being dragged into sin.

First, he considered the long-term cost of a momentary

affair. Joseph was making great strides professionally, especially in light of his young age. Starting as a teenage slave, he had progressed to the top position in one of Egypt's most prominent households. His professional and financial well-being were on the line. Most of us, too, stand to lose significantly if we find ourselves in the clutches of immorality. Our family, reputation, leadership, credibility, and financial stability are all on the line. The implications of sin's grasp are staggering when we stop to count the cost. Joseph looked at the down-side risk and evaluated the potential harm. This practical perspective was the first step in putting on his tear-away jersey.

Second, he remembered that this wouldn't be a sin against his master, the woman, his parents, or himself alone. Joseph realized that immorality is a sin against God. This is not a victimless crime; God is the ultimate victim. Our actions tell God that He has not provided adequately for us, that He is unworthy of our obedience, and that we know more about life than He does.

Outta Here!

We never sin without hurting those around us and that is particularly true of immorality. The result of our moral failure is far-reaching on earth and grievous to heaven.

Joseph's perspective on immorality wasn't based on the fear of being caught nor the wish to avoid a sexually transmitted disease. His main motivation was to maintain his moral purity and to obey God. This sin would have dishonored God, and that was the last thing Joseph wanted to do. Understanding and commitment helped him get the tear-away jersey over his head and prepared him for action.

The action he took was basic, fundamental, and available to any of us: he ran like a scared rabbit. The running backs in their tear-away jerseys had nothing on Joseph. He scrambled out of the temptress' grasp as best he could, leaving his outer cloak in her clutches. He got as much distance between himself and her as possible.

"Flee the evil desires of youth." The story of Joseph was probably on Paul's mind as he penned those words in 2 Timothy 2:22. The price of failure is too high to stand and fight. The best strategy is to make a tactical and hasty retreat.

Let's keep the tear-away jersey close at hand today because the temptations are everywhere. Count the cost, recognize the serious affront that immorality brings to God, and scamper away from the threat like a grid-iron hero heading for pay dirt.

EXTRA POINTS
READ JAMES 1:13-15

- What price would be paid by you, your family, and your friends if you fell into immorality?
- From what temptation in your life do you need to keep running?

TWENTY-SIX

Don't Settle for Driving

In the early years of pro football, Mickey McBride, owner of the Cleveland Browns, had a problem. He had too many good players and not enough room on his active roster for all of them. If he cut some they'd end up playing for one of his opponents and he would miss the chance of seeing them develop their potential. On the other hand, the rules strictly limited the size of the team.

The problem was puzzling but not overwhelming for a resourceful businessman like McBride. After all, he'd made a fortune through his ever-expanding taxicab company. He had faced challenging problems in the past, and his creativity would solve this one as well.

What a coincidence — some of these "almost good enough for the NFL" players became highly paid taxi drivers in Cleveland. While they drove taxis, they waited for a regular player to falter or an injury to open a spot on the team. When the opportunity arose, the taxi job was forgotten, and the player was back in pads.

Interesting Idleness
While the Cleveland players were anxious to get out on the playing field, it seems that some of us Christians might enjoy

life on the taxi squad. Close enough to the game to feel a part of the team, but with enough distance from the action never to get sweaty. We'd avoid the pain, letting someone else be responsible if anything went wrong.

Sadly, this is a huge problem for many churches and ministries. While a few good players are being battered and bruised out on the field, others with excellent qualifications have chosen to stay in the taxi.

Timothy was one who might have enjoyed shouting encouragement to his teammates from the sidelines or the stands. He was gifted, but he was also timid. He had skills to offer but needed support and encouragement to move into front-line action.

Paul was a wise coach who moved Timothy off of the taxi squad into a place of total participation. In 2 Timothy 1:6, Paul commands him:

Fan into flame the gift of God, which is in you through the laying on of my hands.

The spark was there but it needed to be fanned and fed in order to burst into useful flame. Timothy is like many of us. We enjoy having the spark of God's presence in our hearts. The warmth is satisfying and reassuring; it reminds us that we are on the right team. But until it is fanned into flame there is no danger and no demand upon our life.

Engaging Examples

Moving from the taxi squad to the active roster takes courage and commitment. Paul knew that Timothy needed help, so in the next chapter he provided three examples for Timothy to follow as he stepped into the front lines to engage in service. First, he pictures a soldier—

Endure hardship with us like a good soldier. (2:3)

Serving Christ may involve hardship. It takes time to prepare Sunday school lessons; you risk friendship and popularity when confronting a sinful situation. Sharing your faith is often threatening, and helping the needy will put you in some very uncomfortable situations. But a soldier goes on active duty expecting to face tough times. He doesn't sign up for a tour of duty with thoughts of sipping iced tea while lounging beside the pool. If we're to serve God we must expect hardships and not be surprised when they come.

The next picture is of an athlete—

If anyone competes as an athlete, he does not receive the victor's crown unless he competes according to the rules. (2:5)

No one is scrutinized as much as the players on the active roster. Officials watch every move on the field and the press and fans notice everything that happens off the field. Roster players are expected to conduct themselves with honor and integrity. Paul provides Timothy, and us, with fair warning: When you play first team, play by the rules.

The last picture is of a faithful farmer—

The hardworking farmer should be the first to receive a share of the crops. (2:6)

The person who follows God works hard. The soldier and

the athlete have victories to win, but the farmer has nothing but more cows to milk and more fields to plow. The reward for the farmer is much less exotic than the trophies of the soldier or athlete. The farmer must simply be satisfied with a job well done. The additional distinction of the farmer is that he has something edible to show for his efforts. The faithful service of the farmer means productivity. Paul said to Timothy, "I want to see some results when you get into the action."

All of this applies to us today. May we never become comfortable sitting on the taxi squad of the Christian life. We need to find a place of active service and fan into flame our God-given gifts.

EXTRA POINTS
READ 2 THESSALONIANS 3:10-13

- Which of your gifts from God need to be fanned into flame through more active service?
- Which best describes your situation: the soldier, the athlete, or the farmer? Why?

TWENTY-SEVEN

GAME DAY

GAME DAY WAS ALWAYS SPECIAL IN HIGH SCHOOL. WE WORE OUR jerseys and stood up on stage at the pep rally. We ate special food for lunch and met later to go over last-minute adjustments in the game plan. The whole week had prepared us for this day—our time to shine, our moment of truth. We expected to execute the plays with skill and enthusiasm, moving on to our ultimate goal: a victory celebration at McDonald's after the heat of battle.

Players live for game day. When the field lights finally flash on and the band starts pumping out the fight song, it's all business on another Friday night.

The Preparation Is Crucial

Of course, the preceding week is dedicated to recovery, practice, and intense preparation. That's because as soon as one game ends, the cycle begins again—watching films of the last week's game, determining what went right and what needed improvement. Cuts and bruises received daily attention as the focus narrowed to the next opponent.

High school football teams spend a whole week getting ready to be intensely active for two hours on a Friday evening.

For the Christian the reverse is true. Our preparation generally lasts for only a couple hours on Sunday morning while the struggles of the game play out during the rest of the week.

Sadly, many of us think of Sunday as the Christian's game day. We put on our best uniforms, eat special meals, and spend time with other team members. But Sunday isn't when we play the game; rather, it's only the preparation for our "game week." The writer of the book of Hebrews understood the importance of preparation. He recognized that without the training and healing received in our team meetings, success will likely elude us during game week.

Let us not give up meeting together, as some are in the habit of doing. (10:25)

What should happen during these meetings when the church prepares to face its daunting opposition? Acts 2:42 gives us four clues:

They devoted themselves to the apostles' teaching and to the fellowship, to the breaking of bread and to prayer.

When studying Acts it's sometimes hard to know whether all the practices described are patterns for us to follow today. But in this case, the text clearly offers some key components for us to include in our team meetings whenever we gather. These things will help us develop the strength to face the daunting opponents charging at us during the week.

First, we must have teaching (and an eagerness to learn). The time invested on Sunday morning should provide us with deeper insights into God's Word and help us understand how to live life on a daily basis. The Christians in Acts put themselves under the teaching of those who had invested their lives studying the Scriptures and thinking deeply about the implications for their lives.

Fellowship is the second component. We need the continual reminder that we are not alone in the battle. It's wonderful to know that others are facing similar challenges and standing firm. Knowing the strengths and weaknesses of our "teammates," we can encourage and cheer one another on. This happens as we spend time together in conversation and friendship.

The third component, breaking of bread, probably refers to the Lord's Supper. The church needs time to reflect on the price Christ paid to win forgiveness of sins and hope for the future. Remembering His agony and love are central as we prepare to face daily opposition. It is even more reassuring to remember that Christ was *victorious* over sin and death. No matter what the scoreboard says during the middle of the game, we have the confidence that at the end we will be on the winning team.

Last, but not least, is prayer. We are to come together as a unified team to adore God for who He is and to praise Him for what He has done. We can confess our sins and bring our burdens and requests before Him. God isn't like the genie in Aladdin's lamp whom we might control, asking and receiving every request. Rather, God has sought a close and abiding relationship with us. Prayer is our privilege of recognizing His presence and telling Him what is on our minds. Acting beyond our finite understanding, God does what is best for us in each situation, even when He says "no" or "wait."

Ready for Game Week?

In my high school football days, I noticed that the strength of the next opponent determined how seriously we prepared during the week. If we regarded an opponent lightly we might become sloppy in practice and unprepared on game day. When we knew we'd be in a dog fight we paid attention and stayed keenly focused.

The opponents of the believer are powerful and destructive. Use the time of preparation wisely and effectively. Gather regularly with those who will strengthen you to face the challenges of every game week ahead.

EXTRA POINTS
READ MATTHEW 28:16-20

- What changes could you make in your routine to better prepare yourself for Sunday morning worship?
- What challenge are you facing at home or at work that needs special prayer in the coming week?

TWENTY-EIGHT

THE BANQUET: BE THERE!

THE HELMETS HAD BEEN PUT AWAY; JERSEYS LAUNDERED, FOLDED, and stored for next season; combination locks turned in, and playbooks accounted for. Bruises were gone, cuts healed, everyone was walking normally, and all were in a more relaxed mood. The season was over except for the crowning event—the end-of-the-year victory banquet.

No season is complete until the victory banquet. At my ninth-grade banquet I recall the first-year varsity coach searching for words to praise his team, which had suffered through a "perfect" season—nine losses and no wins. I was impressed when he told those of us assembled in the high school cafeteria, "At the first of the season we made tackles and the ball carriers fell forward. By the end of the season they fell backwards." True or not, it made the parents feel a little better and I was impressed that he found anything positive to say about that long season.

The Joy of Completion

As the letters, plaques, and trophies were presented, we always felt pretty good reflecting on the highlights of the past season. Our mistakes didn't look all that tragic, if remembered at all.

We certainly enjoyed the camaraderie and time to reflect on the past with our teammates.

Heaven will be like that. One big end-of-season victory banquet. Bruises, cuts, limps, and pains will be gone, the joy of a completed job will fill the air, highlights will be reviewed, and failures will be irrelevant, if remembered at all.

In fact, Scripture uses the image of a banquet to describe the joy and celebration of the entire life to come.

> *On this mountain the LORD Almighty will prepare a feast of rich food for all peoples, a banquet of aged wine—the best of meats and the finest of wines. . . . He will swallow up death forever. The Sovereign LORD will wipe away the tears from all faces; he will remove the disgrace of his people from all the earth.* (Isaiah 25:6-8)

This party has all three ingredients of a great time: the best host possible, lots of outstanding food and drink, and the ultimate reason to celebrate.

First, the host is God. Some parties survive because there's a great guest list and lively interaction carries the event. Sometimes the entertainment makes it all enjoyable. But truly good parties are the ones that have an outstanding host who makes each guest feel special. The Lord Almighty has invited us as His special guests and He delights in accommodating us in royal fashion. He has prepared the events for our enjoyment, and no detail is left unattended. His greatness and majestic character shine through everywhere we turn. He has honored us beyond our wildest dreams by inviting us to His banquet.

The meal is the best. Wine represents joy and this occasion

is filled with joy at every turn. Laughter fills the air and smiles light up every face. God's abundance and provision are evident in the enormity of the helpings and the quality of the food. The sense of His care and goodness pervades the banquet hall. No one is unsatisfied as the celebration continues.

Finally, recall the reason for the banquet. This is, indeed, a victory celebration. The hard work of the season is past. The bumps and bruises are gone forever. The losses have been converted to victories. The fumbles, interceptions, missed tackles, and dropped passes have been erased from the record book. We are victorious forever. Death has been defeated, tears wiped away, and the disgraces of our lives are forgotten forever. What else can we do but have a party?

Hope is all about planning for the victory banquet at the end of the season of life. For now we are in the battle and we may be in a losing situation. If you are a follower of Christ, take hope. God is preparing a place for you at His victory banquet. Death, tears, and disgrace are our constant companions on this side of the banquet hall door. But hope keeps our eyes fixed on the joy of the party, the victory we celebrate. And most of all, we look forward to close fellowship with the host who has honored us with the greatest of all invitations.

EXTRA POINTS
READ REVELATION 19:6-9

- To what extent are you willing to allow the hope of the future to keep this life's problems in perspective?
- What will be the best thing about God's victory banquet for you?

TWENTY-NINE

TEAM CAPTAINS

ANTICIPATION IS IN THE AIR. THE OPENING PRELIMINARIES ARE finished. The band has played and the twirlers twirled. The anthem has been sung and a small group assembles at midfield meeting with the officials for the coin toss. After perfunctory handshakes the two small groups of team representatives return to their respective sidelines and the game begins.

These representatives are the team captains. Their role is to make decisions for the team and to represent the entire team to the officials. Beyond these limited tasks they are almost indistinguishable from the rest of the team members. They're down in the trenches, making decisions, making mistakes, but sharing in the joys of victory and the sorrows of defeat.

Needed: A Few Good Leaders

Often the team votes on the captains, but sometimes the coaches appoint them. Whatever the selection process, they're chosen because they have great credibility with the other players and they possess the skills of the game. These were two of the qualities of ancient Israel's King David: "[He] shepherded them with integrity of heart; with skillful hands he led them" (Psalm 78:72).

The church desperately needs godly leaders today. But what, exactly, should they be like? We find some crucial leadership qualities coming through in the book of 1 Peter:

Be shepherds of God's flock that is under your care, serving as overseers — not because you must, but because you are willing, as God wants you to be; not greedy for money, but eager to serve; not lording it over those entrusted to you, but being examples to the flock. (5:2-3)

Here are four wonderful qualities for leaders to take on. First, "serving as overseers" means good leaders must be good servants. If we seek a position of authority for ourselves, our integrity has been compromised from the start. Lives that are shallow or lack the fullness that comes from a right relationship with God will look for any substitute to satisfy and fill the void. All too often, a position of leadership is used in exchange for the missing reality. A heart for serving others, and nothing less, is the first requirement for godly leadership.

Second, we must lead because we really want to, not because someone has twisted our arm. A leader filling a position against his will can be expected to do the basics and not much more. But that's not leadership. Leading requires a heart ready and willing to go the extra mile, to make sure the phone calls are made, the plans constructed, the assignments carried out. Without a willing heart there is no true leadership.

Third is the issue of money. Leading with the paycheck in mind is not leading from the heart. In such a case, the skills of the leader will be applied for whoever makes the best offer. This mercenary approach is doomed because true leadership requires a passionate heart. The leader gives his life to accomplish the mission. If dollars are the primary motivation, commitment will wither when the opposition becomes severe.

Peter's final point is that leading primarily means establishing a pattern for others to follow. Leaders don't stand at the back and crack a whip, forcing others forward. They step out in front to create a pathway for the rest. As much as we may want to micro-manage the lives of those around us, we must remember that a good leader creates and champions the "why" of a group and allows his followers to select the best "how."

I am concerned over the lack of leadership in our country, in our churches, and in our homes. At the formation of the United States, strong leaders emerged from a population of about 2.5 million. With well over 250 million in our nation today, we might expect a hundred times as many great leaders. But we look at the world of politics, at business, and even at the church . . . and come away with very few whom we would call true leaders.

What is the solution to this crying need? The answer is simple yet profound: we must each strive to develop integrity of heart and skillfulness of hands. The kingdom-team needs us!

EXTRA POINTS
READ PSALM 78:70-72

- In which arena of leadership are you the strongest—integrity of heart or skillfulness of hand? How do you know?
- Why do you think we have so few great leaders today?

THIRTY

HEADED FOR THE HALL OF FAME?

JIM BROWN, GAYLE SAYERS, BRONCO NEGURSKI, VINCE LOMBARDI, Bob Lilly . . . they're all there in spirit as you walk down the hallowed halls of the Professional Football Hall of Fame in Canton, Ohio. Within this shrine-like facility are housed the greatest memories of pro-football history, along with the tributes and trophies of the men whose exploits built the league.

Being inducted into the Hall of Fame isn't easy. It requires waiting at least five years after your playing career is over; being nominated by a teammate, coach, or fan; surviving a cut to become one of the fifteen finalists, and then receiving an 80 percent favorable vote by a thirty-six-member selection committee. So this is certain: if you're in, you were one great player in your day.

Down-to-Earth Faithfulness

In Hebrews 11 we find the Bible's Hall of Fame. The selection process was simple: God included people who lived by faith. The list isn't all inclusive, of course, but those named provide outstanding examples of living life based on faith.

"Living by faith" is a nice-sounding, spiritual phrase, but I find it tough to understand in a practical sense. What does living by faith look like in everyday life? Fortunately, we can look at the lives of the Hall of Fame inductees and get a down-to-earth picture. Rather than reviewing the entire membership roster, let's just focus on three of the hall of famers: Enoch, Jacob, and Rahab.

Enoch is mentioned only a few times in Scripture but apparently he lived an exemplary life. He enjoyed a warm and personal relationship with God that seemed to have set him apart from the people of his day. The details are sketchy, but we know that God took Enoch directly to heaven without experiencing death.

One Bible teacher explained the event this way: Enoch and God were walking through life together and one day God said, "We're closer to my house than yours. Just come home with me." Enoch was translated from this life to the next without experiencing the pain and suffering that usher most people into eternity. Enoch must have been a very special man. Certainly worthy of the Hall of Fame.

Jacob is another story. He was a rebellious young man who manipulated his brother to gain the greater and more favored inheritance. He deceived his aged and blind father to steal a blessing intended for his twin brother. The defining event of Jacob's life is captured in Genesis 32 when he wrestled with the Lord. During the night Jacob moved his family and possessions to a place of safety because he feared a possible attack from his brother Esau.

So Jacob was left alone, and a man wrestled with him till daybreak. When the man saw that he could not overpower

him, he touched the socket of Jacob's hip so that his hip
was wrenched as he wrestled with the man . . . . Then the
man said, "Your name will no longer be Jacob, but Israel,
because you have struggled with God and with men and
have overcome." (Verses 24-28)

At first Jacob was winning the battle, but then, in an instant, his hip was touched powerfully, and the pain hit him hard. The Lord wins the struggle and Jacob walks with a limp for the rest of his life.

Jacob had fought God all of his life. He had rebelled, cheated, deceived, and manipulated virtually every relationship to gain an advantage. But he had come to a point where he had to decide whether he or the Lord would control his life. The pain of the struggle engulfed him as God won the victory. Every painful step Jacob took for the rest of his life would remind him of the changes God had worked in him.

I find Rahab the most intriguing Hall of Famer on the list. She was a prostitute whose life was radically changed when she recognized God's power and authority over her and her nation. She demonstrated great faith in God by assisting the advanced team of Hebrew spies who entered Jericho just before the walls came crashing down by divine power.

All of the walls fell—except where Rahab was living. All because she recognized God's supremacy and chose to side with Him instead of her friends and neighbors. She exercised faith in God by risking her life to side with Him. And that changed everything about her.

It Takes All Kinds

Three very different people with thoroughly different stories. Enoch's faith was the steady, abiding, unquestioning kind that apparently marked his life from start to finish. Jacob's faith was of the struggling variety. His parents had raised him in a home that honored and worshiped God, but for some reason it took a painful, life-changing moment to redirect his heart to the Lord. Rahab had no understanding of who God was or what He expected from her life. But once she encountered His greatness and power, she conformed her life to His authority.

Walking by faith means fostering a humble and personal relationship with God, as Enoch demonstrated. It means quit fighting God and accept His authority in our lives, as in the case of Jacob. And walking with God means forgetting the sins of the past and sacrificing everything to obey and follow Him as Rahab did.

Walk by faith today and model your life after those who have gone before you into God's Hall of Fame. Surely you are headed there, too.

EXTRA POINTS
READ ROMANS 5:1-4

- Who do you most identify with in your journey of faith—Enoch, Jacob, or Rahab? Why?
- How do you feel about Jacob and Rahab being included in God's Hall of Fame? Would you say that God loves you as you are or as you *should* be?

THIRTY-ONE

FREE ADMISSION

EVERY JOB HAS ITS PERKS, AND MY FATHER'S OCCUPATION AS A HIGH-school football coach provided some of the best. Every year he received free passes to any of the high school sporting events in Portland. Not only could our whole family go to the games, but we got to enter the stadiums through a gate designated especially for those who held the highly coveted passes.

We kept the passes in a special spot on top of the refrigerator and woe to the person who didn't return his pass to its rightful place of honor. Friday nights and Saturday afternoons were filled with playing, coaching, scouting, or just watching high school football, so if the passes weren't in their places, a crisis would ensue. We certainly weren't going to pay money to watch football, especially with the free passes available.

Yes, It's Free

The Christian life is based on a free pass that we cannot earn or purchase at any price.

> *For it is by grace you have been saved, through faith—and this not from yourselves, it is the gift of God—not by works, so that no one can boast.* (Ephesians 2:8-9)

Now consider these four important points related to the free pass that God has given. First, we have been saved by grace. This means that God has provided salvation as a gift because He is a loving God who chose to make us the recipients of His love. God chooses to make us part of His family, even though we don't merit His favor.

Second, we need to respond to this gift through faith. Simply trusting in God and His work on our behalf is the basis for becoming His child. Things keep getting better — God even gives us the faith to respond to the gift He has offered.

Third, this free pass is based solely on God's love for us, not because we have earned this special privilege or have done some great deed to make us worthy of God's gift. Out of the goodness of His heart and the mystery of His will, He gives.

Fourth, gratitude should be the special feeling we enjoy when we accept the gift God has extended to us. Boasting has no place in our hearts.

The Privilege of Sonship

Those football game passes were wonderful, but even better were the times I tagged along with my dad as he scouted an upcoming opponent. Not only would we get into the stadium but we would watch the game from the press box. With clipboard in hand Dad would knock on the press box door, and we'd be welcomed inside by his colleagues who were already sitting in the coaches section. My seat was alongside or just behind my dad. I enjoyed the game from a bird's-eye view and I loved the rush of being an insider. Any other kid knocking on the door would have been shut out and sent away. Not me; I was with my dad and that made all the difference.

I'll never forget the lesson of the press box. The reason I got a pass in the first place was because of my father. The reason I had access to the press box was because of my father. The reason I was treated with dignity was because of my father. Apart from him I was a nobody. With my father I was a privileged son. Paul describes this privilege in Galatians:

> *So you are no longer a slave, but a son; and since you are a son, God has made you also an heir.* (4:7)

We were born with sin as our master, and God provided the free pass. The reason we have left slavery is because of our Father. The reason we have entered His family is because of our Father. The reason we enjoy the benefits of the family is because of our Father. We are Hips sons and along with the new relationship come new privileges and responsibilities.

If you have never accepted His free gift, today would be a great time to do it. From this moment forward you can live life as a son of the God of the universe. In your heart of hearts let Him know that without His free pass of salvation you realize you'll never enter His arena.

EXTRA POINTS
READ ROMANS 6:23.

- Do you know for sure that you have accepted God's free pass of salvation?
- If so, what benefits do you enjoy because you are a child of God?

About the Author

DAN BOLIN IS THE PRESIDENT OF DAN BOLIN RESOURCE, INC., WHICH provides ministry, marketing, management, and fundraising support to Christian nonprofit ministries. He is also a senior associate with the Goehner Resource Group and a regional representative for Christian Camping International.

Dan earned his bachelor's degree from Seattle Pacific University and his master's of theology degree from Dallas Theological Seminary. He also holds an MBA from LeTourneu University.

A frequent speaker both nationally and internationally, Dan is the author or coauthor of several books, including *The One That Got Away, Avoiding the Blitz, How to Be Your Daughter's Daddy, How to Be Your Little Man's Dad,* and *How to Be Your Wife's Best Friend.* He has also been published in *Decision Magazine* and *The Journal of Christian Camping.*

Dan, his wife Cay, and their daughter Haley live near Tyler, Texas, where he serves as an elder at Bethel Bible Church and as a board member of Dan Anderson Ministries and the Tyler Independent School District.

If you liked AVOIDING THE BLITZ, be sure to check out these other men's books from NavPress!

The One That Got Away

This "catchy" devotional based on fishing is perfect
for the guy who loves to fish. Each short devotional highlights
an element of fishing, applying a spiritual truth and lesson for life.
Great for gift giving!

The One That Got Away
(Dan Bolin) $10

Becoming a Man of Prayer

Based on Jesus' instructions, this book will help you pray consistently—
starting with five minutes each day to an hour spent in prayer—and become a
man of prayer. Includes discussion questions.

Becoming a Man of Prayer
(Bob Beltz) $10

Dangers Men Face

Being prepared can make all the difference when it comes to danger.
Learn five common dangers that men face in life and be prepared to deal with
these dangers head-on. Includes discussion questions.

Dangers Men Face
(Jerry White) $14

Get your copies today at your local bookstore, or call
(800) 366-7788 and ask for offer **#2134**.

NAVPRESS
BRINGING TRUTH TO LIFE
www.navpress.com

Prices subject to change without notice.